Somalia and the Changing Nature of Peacekeeping

Somalia and the Changing Nature of Peacekeeping
The Implications for Canada

---

a study prepared for

the Commission

of Inquiry into

the Deployment of

Canadian Forces

to Somalia

Allen G. Sens

```
JX1981.P7 S56 1997
0134/0/00/839
Sens, Allen Gregory,
1964-
Somalia and the changing
nature of peacekeeping
    c1997.
```

© Minister of Public Works and Government Services Canada 1997
Printed and bound in Canada

Available in Canada through
your local bookseller or by mail from
Public Works and Government Services Canada — Publishing
Ottawa, Canada K1A 0S9

Catalogue No. CP32-64/1-1997E
ISBN 0-660-16867-7

Canadian Cataloguing in Publication Data

Sens, Allen Gregory, 1964-

Somalia and the changing nature of peacekeeping :
the implications for Canada

Issued also in French under title: La Somalie et
l'évolution du maintien de la paix.
ISBN 0-660-16867-7
Cat. no. CP32-64/1-1997E

1. Security, International.
2. International police.
3. Canada — Armed Forces.
I. Commission of Inquiry into the Deployment of
Canadian Forces to Somalia.
II. Title.

JX1981.P7S56 1997   327.1'72   C97-980056-0

Contents

INTRODUCTION AND EXECUTIVE SUMMARY ix

CHAPTER ONE — TRADITIONAL PEACEKEEPING DURING THE COLD WAR 1
The United Nations and International Peace and Security 1
    Idealism and Realism: Collective Security and Sovereignty 1
    Idealism and Realism in the Charter: Responsibilities and Limitations 2
    Conflict Management and the UN Charter 5

The United Nations and the Cold War 7
    Collective Security Unfulfilled 7
    The UN Without Collective Security 10

The Birth and Evolution of Peacekeeping 12
    The Early Steps 12
    And So, Peacekeeping 15
    The Conventions of 'Traditional' Peacekeeping 17

Chapter Summary 20

Chronological List of Peacekeeping Missions 22

CHAPTER TWO — THE CHANGING NATURE OF INTERNATIONAL CONFLICT 25
Warfare Since the Second World War 25
    General Trends 25
    The Emergence of Low-Intensity Conflict 26

vi Contents

The End of the Cold War and Ethnic and Religious
Conflicts   28
   The End of the Cold War and Regional Security
   Issues   29
   The Return of History: Ethnic and Religious Conflict
   After the Cold War   30
   The Challenge for Intervention, Management, and
   Conflict Prevention   35

The Future of Armed Conflict   39
   Post-Industrial Warfare/Industrial Warfare   39
   Future Challenges for Conflict Prevention and
   Management   40

Chapter Summary   43

**CHAPTER THREE — THE CHANGING NATURE OF
PEACEKEEPING**   45
The Transition from Cold War to Post-Cold War   45
   The New International Environment: The Role of the UN
   at Fifty   45
   UN Reform and Peacekeeping   46

The Changing Nature of Peacekeeping Missions   50
   The Qualities of Second Generation Peacekeeping   50

Peacekeeping's Time of Troubles: General Implications   53
   The UN and the Credibility Dilemma   53
   Lack of a Suitable Mandate or Doctrine   54
   Increased Great Power Involvement   56
   UN Overstretch and Entrapment   57
   UN Marginalization   59
   Wars of Conscience and the CNN Factor   61
   Future Challenges to PKOs and Operational
   Requirements   64

Chapter Summary   65

CHAPTER FOUR — THE UNITED NATIONS AND SOMALIA: LESSONS AND IMPLICATIONS 69
The Nature of the Conflict in Somalia 69
    The Legacies of the Past: Somalia's History and Social Structure 69
    The Collapse 71
    The Character of the Conflict in Somalia: A Factional Conflict 74

Somalia and Peacemaking and Peacebuilding 75
    The Initial UN Response 75
    The Big Step: UNITAF and UNOSOM II 78
    Somalia as an Example of Peace Enforcement 84

The Lessons of Somalia 85
    The Importance of a Post-Mortem on Somalia 85
    The Potential Contradiction in the Concept of Peacemaking 86
    The Creation of a 'Somalia Syndrome' 88
    The Need to Establish Mechanisms for Dealing with Statelessness 91
    The Decisive Role of the United States 92

Chapter Summary 94

CHAPTER FIVE — PEACEMAKING, THE SOMALIA EXPERIENCE, AND CANADA 97
The Role of Peacekeeping in Canadian Security Policy 97
    Peacekeeping and Canadian Interests 97

Peace Enforcement, Canada, and the Somalia Experience 101
    Peace Enforcement and Canadian Interests 101
    Canada and Peace Enforcement in Somalia 104

After Somalia: Canada and UN Peace Operations 107
    Peace Enforcement and Continued Fiscal Constraints 107

Canada Still Over-Extended   109
Peace Enforcement and Equipment and Training
Requirements   101
Canada, Peace Enforcement, and the United States   112
Public Support: Will the Reservoir of Good Will Run
Dry?   113

Canada and UN Peace Operations: Options for the
Future   114
   The Alternatives for Canada   114

Chapter Summary   120

CHAPTER SIX — CONCLUSIONS   123
General Summary and Conclusions   123
   Core Arguments Made and Central Lessons
Highlighted   123
Implications for the Investigation into the Belet Huen
Incidents   127
Implications for Canada and Future UN Peace
Operations   128

A Final World   129

NOTES   131

Introduction and Executive Summary

This study was commissioned as an independent research project under the auspices of the Commission of Inquiry into the Deployment of Canadian Forces to Somalia (the Somalia Inquiry).[1] The intent of the study is to provide an analysis of the changing nature of United Nations peacekeeping operations (UN PKOs) and the implications for Canadian peacekeeping efforts, with a special emphasis on the Somalia experience. The study examines the wider context for deployment of Canadian Joint Force Somalia (CJFS) to reveal the structural factors or explanations pertinent to the Inquiry's terms of reference. It is not an investigation of specific incidents or activities of the Canadian Airborne Regiment Battle Group (CARBG) and the death and injury of Somali nationals. Rather, it is an examination of the larger issues surrounding UN PKOs and the UN experience in Somalia. This examination is intended to reveal the structural context in which the incidents took place and what role (if any) these structural factors played in the incidents under investigation by the Inquiry.

Accordingly, the study is organized around the following questions:

- What were the conventions of traditional peacekeeping, and how were they rooted in the nature of the Cold War?
- How has the changing nature of conflict affected conflict management efforts and instruments, and how might it continue to do so?
- How have peacekeeping operations changed?
- What are the lessons and implications of the UN effort in Somalia?
- What are the implications of the changing nature of peacekeeping and the Somalia experience for Canada?
- What trends can be identified that have implications for the future of peacekeeping?
- What will be required to respond to these trends?

Each of the five chapters in this study has a clearly defined subject, and each reaches observations and conclusions that build on the discussion in previous chapters. The conclusions are highlighted in the summaries at the end of each chapter.

Chapter 1 examines the development and evolution of traditional UN PKOs and the characteristics that came to define them. The central argument is that traditional peacekeeping was shaped by the character of regional conflicts during the Cold War and by the constraints imposed on the UN system. As an improvised method of conflict management, the conventions of traditional peacekeeping reflected the needs and constraints of the time.

However, Chapter 2 reveals how conflict has evolved since the early days of the Cold War, with a special emphasis on the surge in post-Cold War regional conflicts. The changing qualities of conflict have posed a challenge to existing conflict management instruments, especially peacekeeping, which were developed to manage different types of conflicts under a different set of international conditions. The chapter explores the extent to which future conflicts are likely to acquire new qualities, which must be anticipated as much as possible if conflict management efforts are to be suited to the task of responding to them.

Chapter 3 is devoted to evaluating how UN PKOs have changed in an effort to adapt to the changing qualities of contemporary conflicts identified in Chapter 2. The central theme of the chapter is that operations in the former Yugoslavia, Cambodia and Somalia tried to build on the success of traditional peacekeeping, but in doing so adopted new mandates and methods that created a number of contradictions and inconsistencies between ends and means. The chapter explores the implications of the UN's troubled experience with 'peace enforcement' operations.

Chapter 4 then examines the Somalia mission in greater detail as a case study of the themes outlined in Chapter 3. The chapter highlights several lessons and implications that emerged from this experience with peacekeeping under Chapter VII of the United Nations Charter. The chapter argues that the UN operation mounted in Somalia was seriously flawed in several important respects and goes on to highlight some of the implications of this troubled operation.

Canadian peacekeeping policy is the focus of Chapter 5. The role peacekeeping has played in Canadian foreign and defence policy is explored. The implications of the changing nature of peacekeeping, discussed in Chapter 3, are discussed here in the Canadian context. The Canadian deployment to Somalia is explored, and the implications of the Somalia experience are highlighted. The chapter offers some recommendations for future Canadian involvement in UN peace operations.

The study reaches the following general conclusions:

- The misapplication of force is a serious obstacle to the success of UN PKOs. The attempt to use force to compel, coerce, or otherwise intimidate warring factions in an intrastate conflict, to facilitate the delivery of humanitarian relief supplies, to protect refugee populations, or to terminate hostilities and establish a political resolution is at odds with the United Nations' ability to act as an instrument of peace and stability. In attempting to rectify one of the perceived deficiencies of UN PKOs in 'less permissive' environments — the lack of sufficient force — the UN has undercut many of the other elements that enabled UN PKOs to be effective. Force can be an effective instrument when it is applied in a discriminate and calibrated fashion in support of a coherent mission plan and an effective political process, but this did not occur in Somalia.
- The changing nature of armed conflict has had fundamental implications for the conduct of UN PKOs and will continue to do so in the future. UN PKOs will continue to encounter an ever-widening range of threats and tasks. Foremost among these will be encounters with different forms of intrastate conflict, ever more sophisticated weapons systems, the advent of information warfare, chemical and biological warfare, and attacks on contributing countries. A key to the success of future UN operations will be the extent to which these and other new challenges are anticipated and prepared for.
- Canada's peacekeeping policy has been affected by the changed nature of peacekeeping and the reality of domestic fiscal constraints. Nevertheless, Canada should continue to participate in UN operations. At the same time, however, Canada must take steps to reduce the overstretch of the Canadian Armed Forces. To reconcile demand with limited resources, Canada should enhance its capacity to deploy smaller military and/or civilian formations with specialized capabilities to fill niche roles within UN missions when regular infantry formations are not available for expeditionary missions. Furthermore, although military training provides the essential foundation, or prerequisite, for effective peacekeepers, the expanding range of threats and tasks and the localized nature of contemporary conflicts require that peacekeeping training and mission-specific training be enhanced.

- The incidents under investigation by the Somalia Inquiry cannot be explained fully or adequately by the structural or contextual factors examined in this study. Explanations derived from the individual or group level of analysis would be more effective in establishing the immediate causes of these incidents. However, the study concludes that structural factors did play a role in creating the conditions for (or the permissive causes of) the incidents under investigation, in the form of the overstretch of the Canadian Armed Forces in the face of the demand for peacekeeping contingents.

CHAPTER ONE

Traditional Peacekeeping During the Cold War

THE UNITED NATIONS AND INTERNATIONAL PEACE AND SECURITY

Idealism and Realism: Collective Security and Sovereignty

The Early Context. The origins of the United Nations lie in the early planning for a postwar international organization and agencies, most of which was conducted in Great Britain and the United States.[1] However, serious preparations at the political level, and the beginning of international diplomatic activity on the issue of the postwar order, did not begin until 1943. At a conference in Moscow in October of that year, the Allied Powers committed themselves to the creation of a general international organization at the conclusion of the war. In the period between the Moscow Conference and the beginning of the construction of a new international organization at Dumbarton Oaks on 21 August 1944, a number of functional international agencies were established to prepare for the requirements of the postwar system and lay the groundwork for international co-operation on these requirements.[2] Subsequent to Dumbarton Oaks, and after a consultation during the Yalta Conference in February 1945, a general conference — the United Nations Conference on International Organization — of the allied war effort was convened at San Francisco on 25 April 1945. Fifty countries attended the conference, and the proposals of the Big Three were debated and modified to produce a draft of the Charter of the United Nations and the Statute of the International Court of Justice. The Charter of the United Nations was signed in San Francisco on 26 June 1945 at the conclusion of the United Nations Conference on International Organization and came into force on 24 October 1945. The first session of the General Assembly commenced in London on 10 January 1946.

The Security Imperative of the United Nations. From its inception, the United Nations was first and foremost a security institution.[3] However, it was not intended to be a security organization to the exclusion of other roles and functions, although both Great Britain and the Soviet Union would have been satisfied with such a focus. Largely at the insistence of the United States, the UN was conceived and designed to address a wide range of issues and problems, including human rights, international law, cultural and humanitarian issues, and the promotion of economic and social progress. These objectives were all enshrined in the preamble and in article 1 of the UN Charter. The structure of the UN also reflects this vision: the Economic and Social Council and the Trusteeship Council are designated, along with the Security Council, the International Court of Justice, and the Secretariat, as the "principle organs" of the UN. The UN also has many specialized agencies working in the development, human rights, and social and economic spheres. However, the principle rationale for the creation of the UN was to establish an instrument of peace and security for the postwar world. As stated in the first sentence of the preamble to the Charter, the UN was intended to "save succeeding generations from the scourge of war." The first article of the first chapter of the UN Charter, under the heading "Purposes of the United Nations", states that the UN is to

maintain international peace and security, and to that end: to take effective collective measures for the prevention and removal of threats to the peace, and for the suppression of acts of aggression or other breaches of the peace, and to bring about by peaceful means, and in conformity with the principles of justice and international law, adjustment or settlement of international disputes or situations which might lead to a breach of the peace;[4]

The security dimension was paramount in the minds of the UN's creators. They were not, however, entirely sanguine about the ability of the UN to achieve this task; the UN Charter is laced with a heavy dose of realism.

Idealism and Realism in the Charter: Responsibilities and Limitations

Collective Security and the Right of Self-Defence. The UN Charter strikes a precarious balance between idealistic hopes and realistic antidotes. This was a direct consequence of both the hopes of the time and perceived limits imposed by an anarchical international system. The UN system was intended to be a collective security system, whereby any aggression by a member state (or any state outside the UN system) would be met with the combined resistance of all other members of the system. In such an 'all against one' system, the prospect of confronting this preponderance of force would deter states from embarking on campaigns of aggression. Furthermore, joining the UN committed member states to settle their international disputes through peaceful means, and to "refrain in their international relations from the threat or use of force against the territorial integrity or political independence of any state, or in any other manner inconsistent with the Purposes of the United Nations."[5] Instead, states were to rely on the UN's responsibility to maintain international peace and security, through the use of force if this became necessary. Despite this vision, other provisions of the UN Charter reflect scepticism about the UN's ability to perform this task. States retain the right of individual self-defence under article 51, which reads:

Nothing in the present Charter shall impair the inherent right of individual or collective self-defence if an armed attack occurs against a Member of the United Nations, until the Security Council has taken measures necessary to maintain international peace and security. Measures taken by Members in the exercise of this right of self-defence shall be immediately reported to the Security Council and shall not in any way affect the authority and responsibility of the Security Council under the present Charter to take at any time such action as it deems necessary in order to maintain or restore international peace and security.[6]

Further, under article 52, states have the right to engage in regional efforts to enhance their security:

Nothing in the present Charter precludes the existence of regional arrangements or agencies for dealing with such matters relating to the maintenance of international peace and security as are appropriate for regional action, provided that such arrangements or agencies and their activities are consistent with the Purposes and Principles of the United Nations.[7]

The UN was not, therefore, given exclusive responsibility for the defence of its members; that states were accorded the individual and collective right to self-defence was a reflection of the recognized limitations of the UN.

The Sovereign Equality of States and the Permanent Five. Another prominent example of the compromise between idealism and realism in the Charter is the principle of equality and the special status of the permanent members of the Security Council. The UN system was built on the principle that all states, regardless of size, power, or location in the world, were equal in sovereign rights. As article 2/1 states: "The Organization is based on the principle of the sovereign equality of all its Members."[8] However, the drafters of the UN Charter were well aware that this principle did not extend far into the practicalities of international life; some states were clearly more important than others, and the special privileges accorded the Permanent Five (P5) in the Security Council reflected that judgement. Furthermore, the membership of the P5 reflected the power realities in place at the end of the Second World War. The drafters of the UN Charter regarded the unity of the great powers as essential for the maintenance of world peace, for no action by the UN could be effective without the support of the great powers. As Inis R. Claude, Jr. has put it, "The Charter registered power; it did not confer it."[9] This has brought two criticisms down on the UN: first, the privileges of the P5 enhanced the power of these states, so the UN became a vehicle for the aggrandizement of the great powers, particularly as the Security Council was given primary responsibility for maintaining international peace and security on behalf of the UN membership; and second, the composition of the Security Council has become increasingly outdated and no longer reflects current realities.[10]

International Peace and Security and Internal Sovereignty. The UN system is built around the state as the central unit in international relations. Membership, after all, is open to all (peace-loving) states; no other unit is mentioned in the Charter as a potential candidate for this status. The principle of state sovereignty is enshrined in the Charter in article 2/7:

Nothing contained in the present Charter shall authorize the United Nations to intervene in matters which are essentially within the domestic jurisdiction of any state or shall require the Members to submit such matters to settlement under the present Charter; but this principle shall not prejudice the application of enforcement measures under Chapter VII.[11]

The internal sovereignty principle is not especially airtight in the Charter, however, and there are many ambiguities — largely intentional — in the Charter and in UN resolutions that challenge the universal applicability of internal sovereignty.

- First, as stated in article 2/7, invoking Chapter VII enforcement measures overrides the right of a state to invoke the sovereignty provision.
- Second, the principle of internal sovereignty applies only to matters "essentially within" the domestic jurisdiction of states. If it is determined that a matter does not lie within this jurisdiction, then article 2/7 does not apply.[12]
- Third, the functions of the UN Charter contained in Chapters IX and X (which cover international economic and social co-operation in human rights, social and economic development, and culture and education and the Economic and Social Council) are largely inconsistent with the principle of non-intervention in matters of domestic jurisdiction.
- Fourth, UN resolutions have challenged this principle. In 1970, the UN General Assembly passed a resolution that read:

Every State has the duty to refrain from any forcible action which deprives peoples ... of their right of self-determination and freedom and independence. In their actions against, and resistance to, such forcible action in pursuit of the exercise of their right to self-determination, such peoples are entitled to seek and to receive support in accordance with the purposes and principles of the Charter.[13]

The idealist/realist compromises in the UN Charter are also reflected in the provisions for the settlement of disputes, which are divided between Chapter VI and Chapter VII of the UN Charter.

Conflict Management and the UN Charter

Chapter VI: Pacific Settlement of Disputes. The drafters of the UN Charter placed great hope in a world where disputes would be resolved by means short of violence. However, the foundation of the collective security system they sought to install is based on the threat of force wielded by the UN. The drafters of the Charter divided these components of the UN system into two separate chapters, reflecting not only the different nature of their provisions but also the fundamental divergence between them. Chapter VI of the UN Charter, entitled "Pacific Settlement of Disputes", outlines the obligations of member states and the responsibilities of the UN Security Council with respect to international disputes. In the event of a dispute between states, Chapter VI calls on the parties to seek a resolution through "negotiation, enquiry, mediation, conciliation, arbitration, judicial settlement, resort to regional agencies or arrangements, or other peaceful means of their own choice."[14] The Security Council is able to investigate the dispute to determine whether it constitutes a danger to international peace and security, and in that eventuality make recommendations with respect to procedures or methods of resolution. The Security Council can also make itself available to the parties to assist in the resolution of the dispute, provided all the parties to a dispute make a request to that effect. In Chapter VI rest several important conventions about the role of the UN as a conflict resolution mechanism: it is meant to act as a facilitator of peaceful resolutions to disputes; it acts as an impartial third party; and it can act only with the consent of the parties to a dispute.

Conflict Management and Chapter VII: Threats to the Peace. The collective security mission of the UN is entrenched in Chapter VII, entitled "Action with Respect to Threats to the Peace, Breaches of the Peace, and Acts of Aggression". Although the provisions for the use of force by the UN dominate Chapter VII, actions other than the use of force are also contained in this chapter. Under articles 40 and 41, the Security Council can call on the parties to comply with provisional measures agreed to by the Security Council, then call on member states to observe a number of measures not involving the use of armed force, commonly referred to as sanctions. If these measures prove inadequate, the Security Council can invoke article 42:

Should the Security Council consider that measures provided for in Article 41 would be inadequate or have proved to be inadequate, it may take such action by air, sea, or land forces as may be necessary to maintain or restore international peace and security. Such action may include demonstrations, blockade, and other operations by air, sea, or land forces of Members of the United Nations.[15]

Chapter VII also specifies the obligation of member states with respect to UN Security Council actions under article 42, including the provision of forces, facilities, and transit rights, subject to previous consultation with the Security Council. Chapter VII also establishes the modalities for the use of force by the UN: the UN must rely on contributions from member states to field military forces; the UN was to have no army of its own;

planning and control of such operations were to be handled by the UN by means of the Military Staff Committee; and co-ordination and planning were to be established between the UN and its member states for such eventualities.

THE UNITED NATIONS AND THE COLD WAR

Collective Security Unfulfilled

Great Power Disunity and the Effectiveness of the UN. The onset of the Cold War had a profound impact on the UN. The first and most fundamental consequence was the inability of the organization to perform its core security function, that of collective security for its members. The breakdown of the Second World War alliance and the souring of relations among the great powers condemned the Security Council not to complete irrelevance, but to collective action only on issues that the deeply divided governments of the P5 could agree upon. This eventuality had been anticipated, for during the Second World War there was an understanding that the UN would work only if good relations persisted between the great powers; a serious division among them would spell disaster for the new organization. The drafters of the UN Charter could see an onrushing train that would destroy the efficacy of the UN, yet they were powerless to stop it. The UN itself could not create a co-operative relationship among the great powers; as U.S. secretary of state Cordell Hull argued, "no machinery, as such, can produce this essential harmony and unity."[16] The UN was built on the assumption that great power unity was essential for the effective management of global affairs, including international peace and security. It was understood that if this did not exist, the UN would be largely unable to perform this task as its designers envisioned. It did not take long for these concerns to prove well founded.

The Military Staff Committee and the Failure of Collective Security. The collective security arrangements in the Charter were an early casualty of great power disunity in the Security Council. Essential to the planning, preparation, and formation of the UN's collective security military muscle was the Military Staff Committee (MSC):

There shall be established a Military Staff Committee to advise and assist the Security Council on all questions relating to the Security Council's military requirements for the maintenance of international peace and security, the employment and command of forces placed at its disposal, the regulation of armaments, and possible disarmament.[17]

The MSC was therefore responsible for the conduct of article 42 operations under Chapter VII of the Charter. However, the MSC foundered over the national disagreements and lack of enthusiasm for such arrangements that attended the Cold War and failed to construct any agreements on the commitment of member states' armed forces to the UN under Article 42.[18] The issue was shelved in 1948, and although numerous proposals have been made for reinvigorating the MSC, it continues to this day to be an empty shell of what it was intended to be. The failure of the MSC is a reflection of what has been called the "slow death" of the collective security mission of the UN, the very foundation of the UN system as envisaged by its creators.[19]

Korea: The Great Anomaly. The experience in Korea revealed two lessons about the nature of the UN in the Cold War world. First, the Security Council did act in response to the North Korean invasion of South Korea in June 1950, but it was able to do so only in the absence of the Russian delegation. Without the Russians present to exercise their veto, the Security Council condemned the invasion, called on member states to assist South Korea, and established a unified command to co-ordinate the effort against North Korea. This was a vivid reminder of the extent to which the Cold War defined the capability of the Security Council to act in the realm of peace and security.

Second, while it is true that U.S. leadership was vital in the international response to North Korean aggression, the UN was effectively marginalized in the Korean War by the government of the United States, to the point of being used by the United States as an instrument to obtain international support for a primarily U.S. operation. Despite the existence of a UN command, the UN did not establish either effective political coordination of the effort or operational command and control over UN-flagged forces in the field. Furthermore, the bulk of these forces were in fact American; the United States contributed approximately half the ground forces (only about 10 per cent of the UN force in Korea was non-American or non-Korean), and the vast majority of air and naval power. This was a lesson that was to resurface for the UN: the danger of losing political and operational control of a UN mission to a great power.

The Uniting for Peace Resolution. The lessons of the Korean experience — particularly the first lesson — led to the Uniting for Peace Resolution passed by the UN General Assembly in November 1950. The resolution provided for the assumption by the General Assembly of responsibility for matters concerning international peace and security in the event that the Security Council was unable to act. It was recognized that such an action would have serious consequences for the UN. It would involve a change to the provisions and mechanisms contained in the Charter (particularly those covering responsibility for maintaining international peace and security), and it would place increased demands on the General Assembly. To examine these consequences and determine how they might be addressed, the Uniting for Peace Resolution created the Collective Measures Committee (CMC), called on member states to provide information on the contributions they would be willing to make to UN operations, and created a military panel to act as a liaison between the UN and member states on force compatibility and training. However, the efforts of the Uniting for Peace Resolution and the CMC came to naught, largely because member states proved unwilling to contribute to or cooperate with these initiatives. The reality of the Cold War and national sovereignty over armed force foiled this effort to circumvent the Security Council.

Regional Security and Collective Defence Dominates. The onset of the Cold War also saw the development of regional arrangements based not on the principles of collective security, but on the principles of collective defence.[20] Although they drew their legitimacy at least in part from article 52 of the UN Charter, these arrangements were traditional alliances, aimed at a specific threat. Member states' lack of faith and confidence in the collective security provisions was reflected in the devotion of resources to these alliances and the lack of devotion of these resources to the UN. The western alliance system, established and managed by the United States, was built on the North Atlantic Treaty Organization (NATO), founded in 1949, and the close security relationship between Washington and Tokyo. Other regional efforts were made, most notably in the Middle East and Asia, where the Baghdad Pact (and later the Central Treaty Organization, CENTO) and the South East Asian Treaty Organization (SEATO) respectively were built around U.S. initiatives directed against the Soviet Union. Although neither CENTO nor SEATO was very effective (SEATO was dissolved in 1977, and CENTO suffered the same fate in 1979), they demonstrated the route that states had chosen with respect to their own security and global security arrangements. Collective security under the UN had fallen victim to the Cold War; the UN would have to find its peace and security role elsewhere.

The UN Without Collective Security

The Tower of Babel? The 'Paralysis' of the UN. As its collective security function faded into the background, the UN came to be associated with other functions and roles, some of which were anticipated and intended by its drafters, and some of which were not. The UN swiftly became a key forum for both public and private diplomacy. UN supporters suggested that the UN was an important safety valve, where grievances and misunderstandings could be aired and even resolved. As a global institution, the UN possessed a moral authority or weight that attended its near-universal membership. Resolutions of the UN were therefore an important expression of 'world opinion' on a wide range of issues. However, this role drew criticism, as the UN was disparaged as a mere stage for posturing or theatrics, or another arena in which the superpower conflict was played out. The UN was marginalized, as the creation of other venues for diplomatic activity on security and economic issues proliferated, reducing the significance of the UN system. These included superpower summitry, the Group of Seven, and regional organizations or associations such as the European Communities. Superpower politics and marginalization had frozen the UN's ability to act when it most needed to act. UN paralysis was evident in the prolific use of the veto mechanism by the P5; between 1946 and 1987, the Soviet Union cast 121 vetoes, the United States 58, Great Britain 27, China 22, and France 16. UN paralysis was also evident in the number of conflicts never addressed formally at the UN. These included conflicts in Biafra, Bangladesh, Laos, Cambodia, Sudan, Burma, Chad, Ethiopia, and Lebanon (1975-76). The diplomatic role, although valued, was denigrated as emblematic of the UN's ability to talk but inability to act.

Decolonization. The Second World War sounded the death knell for European colonialism. Although many European colonial powers would continue to hold onto the vestiges of empire, the war left most European powers exhausted and unable or unwilling to combat the rising tide of nationalism and desire for self-determination in many of their colonies.

Others could not expend the resources to recapture or reassert control over colonies conquered during the war. And there was an increasing sentiment that colonies and empires were anachronisms whose time had passed. The impact of decolonization on the international system and the UN system was electric. Membership in the UN grew from 51 states at its inception to 127 by 1970. Regional representation at the UN also changed dramatically. At its inception, the UN had 20 states from Latin America, 9 from Asia and the Middle East, and 2 from Africa. By 1970 there were 40 African members of the UN and 30 from Asia and the Middle East.[21] In two decades, one-third of the world's population gained independence from colonial rule, and by 1970 two-thirds of the membership of the UN was made up of developing countries. From the late 1950s to the early 1970s, colonial issues dominated the UN agenda, and the UN became a venue — and a highly public one — for venting grievances of the poor South against the wealthy North. The flavour of the UN, particularly the General Assembly, changed as criticism was directed at the great powers, especially the United States. The sentiments of the developing world were hostile to the order created by the great powers. This order was seen as "a threat to peace and security because it perpetuates hegemony and dependence, justifies intervention, sanctions racism, frustrates development, and fosters the conditions that breed disorder and violence."[22] The UN played an important role in decolonization, often acting as a mediator, supplying observers for larger peacekeeping missions, and giving the new states a forum to air their views. However, there were significant negative consequences as well. The criticism of the developing countries alienated the United States, especially as many of these states began to fall (or were perceived as falling) into the Soviet camp. The North/South split also created acrimony and disunity on other issues such as South Africa and disarmament. Finally, the decolonization experience became associated with the superpower rivalry, as the United States and the Soviet Union competed for influence and allies and fought proxy wars in the Middle East, Asia, and Africa.

The UN and 'Functional' Roles. The UN was conceived as an organization that would perform a variety of economic, social, and technical functions. The Economic and Social Council (ECOSOC) was, after all, one of the principal organs of the UN system. These functions took on a greater visibility and prominence as the security ambitions of the organization were compromised. The UN has played a major role in the process of development. The World Bank and the United Nations Development Program (UNDP) dispensed financial assistance and aid to developing countries. The UN Conference on Trade and Development (UNCTAD) addressed issues related to the place of developing countries in the global trading system. The United Nations Industrial Development Organization (UNIDO) was created to assist countries with their industrial development strategies. The UN also addressed other issues such as narcotics trafficking, refugees (the International Refugee Organization was replaced by the UN High Commissioner for Refugees (UNHCR) in 1961) population, the environment, and human rights. The UN has also become a preferred forum for discussion of a variety of technical issues, including outer space, the sea-bed, and satellites. Defenders of the UN find an important buttress of support for the UN in these functions, although they have been for the most part less visible than the attempts to use the UN for matters pertaining to international peace and security.

THE BIRTH AND EVOLUTION OF PEACEKEEPING

The Early Steps

Finding a Security Role. UN PKOs did not develop in an historical vacuum. The origins of UN peacekeeping can be traced to the experience of the League of Nations, which carried out a wide range of mediation efforts, security and maintenance of order functions, and observer and truce supervision missions. The League experience established the principles of impartiality and the use of minimum force while maintaining or restoring order. A body of experience and some conceptual development were already in place as a result.[23] The Greek Civil War prompted the UN General Assembly (circumventing the Soviet veto) to adopt a U.S. resolution in October 1947 to send an observer mission, under a Special Committee on the Balkans (UNSCOB), of some 35 personnel to Greece to determine whether the insurgents were receiving aid from Greece's Communist neighbours.[24] Because of the Soviet Union's opposition, the observer mission was deployed only on the Greek side of the frontier to survey, inspect, and report on activities along the border. The operation was concluded in 1954, having found ample evidence that aid was being passed across the frontier. UNSCOB was directed against the Soviet Union and its allies and stands as one of the first example of the United States exerting geopolitical aims through the UN. Nevertheless, from a technical standpoint much was learned about the formation, deployment, and principles of conduct of observers in the field. In Indonesia, the UN facilitated the cessation of hostilities and monitored the withdrawal of the Netherlands from its former colony. A Good Offices Committee was established in 1947, and a Commission for Indonesia was established in January 1949. Politically, both the United Nations and the United States placed pressure on the Netherlands to withdraw. In technical terms, the UN assisted with mediation, implementation, and supervision of the ceasefire and withdrawal agreements until this was completed in 1951. These missions are not formally recognized as official UN observer or truce supervisory missions, but they represent the beginning of this role for the UN in the realm of international peace and security.[25]

Peacekeeping Takes Shape: UNTSO, UNMOGIP, and UNEF I. Following the 1948 Arab-Israeli War, the UN established the United Nations Truce Supervisory Organization (UNTSO) in June 1948 to supervise and observe the truce in Palestine. UNTSO's mandate included investigating incidents, confidence-building measures at the local level, defusing tensions and incidents of violence, and acting as a conduit of communication between the parties, who had little or no diplomatic contact between them. UNTSO also performed tasks with subsequent UN missions in the Middle East and currently has an operational strength of 220 personnel.[26]

A similar mission was assigned to the United Nations Military Observer Group in India and Pakistan (UNMOGIP) in the wake of UN mediation that achieved a ceasefire between the two countries. UNMOGIP was launched in January 1949 and investigated incidents, provided information on troop movements, and helped local authorities maintain order and calm. It currently has an operational strength of 40.

The first 'true' peacekeeping operation, however, was the First United Nations Emergency Force (UNEF I), launched on 4 November 1956 under UN General Assembly Resolution 998.[27] This was in response to the Suez crisis, sparked by the nationalization of the Suez Canal by Egypt and the subsequent intervention by Great Britain and France. The mission's mandate was to secure and supervise the cessation of hostilities, observe and facilitate the withdrawal of France, Great Britain, and Israel from Egyptian territory, and serve as a buffer between Egyptian and Israeli forces. UNEF I was under the direction of the Secretary-General of the United Nations and under the command of a neutral officer rather than national commanders. No great powers were involved, and the force was neutral in composition and action. It was from these early experiences that the operational context of what has come to be called 'traditional peacekeeping' was formed. Significantly, UNEF I was to be among the exceptions in the UN peacekeeping record as an example of peacekeeping in an international rather than an internal conflict.

Increasing Experience and Growing Pains: The Congo. In the following years, the UN launched numerous peacekeeping operations, which slowly established a record of experience and lessons built on the beginnings established by UNEF I and the early observer missions. (For a chronological list of UN peacekeeping operations, see page 22.) However, one operation — the United Nations Operation in the Congo — stood out as an exception to the general rules that were beginning to emerge with respect to the design of peacekeeping missions and served to influence the design of future missions. The crisis in the Congo began with its independence from Belgium on 30 June 1960. Independence was granted before stable government and state instruments were established, and rivalries between local factions resulted in increasing anarchy. In response, 10,000 Belgian paratroopers moved into the cities to protect Belgian nationals, although locals suspected that Belgium was attempting to reassert control over the country. At the same time, Katanga province declared its independence from Congo. At the request of the Congolese government, the UN Security Council voted on 14 July 1960 to establish the Opération des Nations Unies au Congo (ONUC). ONUC's initial mandate was to assure the withdrawal of Belgian forces, restore and maintain law and order, and provide technical assistance. Despite the deployment of ONUC, the situation deteriorated as violence spread and intensified to the point of all-out civil war. The superpowers energetically backed their chosen factions. Katanga refused to reintegrate and employed mercenaries in its forces. ONUC personnel also came under attack. In response to this situation, the mandate of ONUC was expanded twice in 1961, to include maintaining the territorial integrity of the Congo, preventing the occurrence of civil war, and securing the withdrawal of all foreign military and advisory personnel not under UN command and all mercenaries. The size of the force was expanded to just under 20,000. At this point, some countries withdrew from ONUC out of concern about the course of events, and ONUC began to be regarded locally as an effort by the UN to assert control over the country. Eventually, as assassinations and exhaustion took their toll, a peace settlement was reached, and the situation stabilized. ONUC was withdrawn in June 1964.

The Lessons and Impact of ONUC. The experience in the Congo left a dark cloud over the UN and many of its member states. Although the mission ended with some semblance of stability and governance reestablished in the Congo, there was a widespread belief that ONUC had been both quagmire and fiasco. The operation had failed to achieve its essential goals and resulted in an unintended and unanticipated escalation of UN involvement. The Congo operation dampened enthusiasm for peacekeeping, both at UN headquarters and among member states, and a brief hiatus ensued before the next UN peacekeeping mission was established in late 1962. There was scepticism about the UN's ability to establish law and order in anarchic internal environments. Subsequent UN peacekeeping missions had very cautious and short-term mandates, in an effort to avoid a replay of the Congo situation. In addition, there was a backlash against the financial demands of UN peacekeeping that was to leave a long legacy of fiscal shortfalls. Many of the experiences of ONUC were to be replayed in Somalia and other UN operations less than three decades later. One of the lessons of the Congo for contemporary peacekeeping debates is that after efforts to stretch the mandate have resulted in negative experiences, future efforts will be carefully bounded and managed. Peacekeeping did survive as a useful and effective device after the bitterness of the Congo experience had faded.

And So, Peacekeeping

The Constraints: The UN System and the Nature of Global Conflict. It was in this global and institutional environment that the UN developed a security role quite unlike that envisioned by its creators. The superpower rivalry and the reality of the veto meant that any security-related function had to pass muster in the Security Council. While the General Assembly initially provided a way of circumventing the Security Council, decolonization and the consequent development of a General Assembly broadly unsympathetic to the West meant that the General Assembly was also split on security issues. The protection accorded to the state and the sovereignty of the state, as well as an international agenda dominated by conflicts between states or between colonial powers and aspirant states, meant that the UN had to respect many principles concerning the supremacy of the state in international affairs. UN peacekeeping operations therefore developed under extraordinarily constrained and bounded circumstances, circumstances that conditioned the nature and quality of peacekeeping operations. These operations occupied a middle ground between the provisions for peaceful resolution of disputes in Chapter VI of the Charter and the enforcement mechanisms (including provisions for the use of force) in Chapter VII. Out of this middle ground was born the formal legal foundation of peacekeeping, the ethereal "Chapter Six-and-a-half" described by former Secretary-General Dag Hammarskjold.[28]

These 'traditional' peacekeeping missions, as they are now referred to, were improvised out of necessity, as a response to the need for a conflict management mechanism for regional conflicts after the Second World War.

Peacekeeping Recognized as the UN's Security Role. When UN peacekeepers won the Nobel Peace Prize in 1988, it was a symbolic reaffirmation of a general international consensus that peacekeeping had performed a useful and by and large successful service to international peace and security. There was, perhaps, an unspoken irony behind the award: that of all the functions and services of the UN, it was peacekeeping — which was neither mentioned in the UN Charter nor envisioned by the organization's creators — that was given special honours for its contribution to the core mission of the institution. Nevertheless, the Nobel Peace Prize also reaffirmed another generally held consensus: that peacekeeping had become the most prominent and visible component of UN operations. For an enterprise not specified in the UN Charter, peacekeeping had become remarkably habitual. From 1948 to 1993, the UN embarked on 28 peacekeeping operations, involving more than 600,000 soldiers.[29] Media coverage of the UN tended to focus on the peacekeeping exploits of the organization, while the other sectors of activity that constituted the bulk of UN operations were less publicized.

Definitions. As peacekeeping is not mentioned in the UN Charter, and as it occupies a vague legal middle ground between the provisions of Chapter VI and Chapter VII of the Charter, there is no standard definition of the term peacekeeping. Some examples include the following:

The prevention, containment, moderation and termination of hostilities between or within states through the medium of third party intervention, organized and directed internationally, using multinational military, police and civilian personnel to restore and maintain peace.

General Indar Jit Riktye
former President, International Peace Academy

United Nations Field operations in which international personnel, civilian and/or military, are deployed with the consent of the parties and under United Nations command to help control or resolve actual or potential international conflicts or internal conflicts which have a clear international dimension.

Marrack Goulding
UN Under-Secretary General for Peacekeeping Operations

17   Traditional Peacekeeping During the Cold War

...any international effort involving an operational component to promote the termination of armed conflict or the resolution of longstanding disputes.

Paul F. Diehl

Actions designed to enhance international peace, security and stability which are authorized and coordinated by competent national and international organizations and which are undertaken cooperatively by military, humanitarian, good governance, civilian police, and other interested agencies and groups.

Alex Morrison, President
Canadian International Peacekeeping Training Centre

These definitions reflect how peacekeeping has evolved to encompass a wider range of mission, tasks and components. Although a standard definition proved elusive, over time UN peacekeeping efforts acquired a set of characteristics or qualities that came to define the parameters and operational modalities of peacekeeping operations.

The Conventions of 'Traditional' Peacekeeping

Impartiality. The impartiality, or neutrality, of UN peacekeeping contingents was of fundamental importance. No side could be seen as being favoured by the UN mission, either among the parties to a conflict or among the member states of the UN itself. Unlike Chapter VII collective security operations, which identified an aggressor, UN PKOs did not presuppose responsibility or identify an aggressor (although the UN can pass judgement on specific actions or condemn one party for those actions). Not only was impartiality essential if the parties to a conflict were to find the deployment of UN peacekeeping contingents acceptable, but maintaining a perception of impartiality was essential to the conflict management functions of the mission. Observation, interposition, fact finding, third-party mediation, and local level negotiation and arbitration tasks could be carried out only if the impartiality of UN peacekeepers was accepted and maintained.

Non-Hostile and Lightly Armed. UN peacekeeping missions were not deployed to embark on offensive military operations. If they were to perform their function as impartial observers and interpositionary forces, and if local parties were to have confidence in their capacity to act as mediators and facilitators, UN peacekeepers could not be regarded as a coercive force, able to achieve these goals through military means. To this end, UN peacekeeping forces were deployed and structured in a non-threatening manner, lacking the traditional military disposition of forces for combat operations, such as strategic depth, reserves, concentration of force, and numerical superiority. UN peacekeepers were also lightly armed, equipped only for self-defence. UN contingents were seldom deployed with their full complement of high-intensity conflict assets and were not supplied for sustained military operations.

Consent. Respect for state sovereignty, enshrined in the UN Charter, required the UN to seek and obtain approval from the parties to a conflict before deploying a peacekeeping force. In addition, the consent of the parties was required to maintain the force; if consent was withdrawn, UN contingents were obliged to leave. This was consistent with the impartial and non-hostile nature of a UN peacekeeping operation and a crucial component of the acceptability of a UN presence. In essence, the parties to a conflict became partners in the UN effort. This ensured not only that a UN force would be deployed in areas where its presence was sanctioned, but also that the environment was one in which lightly armed contingents could perform their tasks. These three measures were interrelated and self-reinforcing and constituted the core of the concept of traditional peacekeeping.

Peacekeeping Operations Could Not Make Peace. UN PKOs did not, and could not, create the conditions for their own success; these conditions had to exist before a UN operation was mounted. In this sense, peacekeeping operations were reactive to a conflict and its peace process, rather than preventive or proactive. UN peacekeeping missions, therefore, were secondary to the wider political process of diplomacy, mediation, and reconciliation between the parties to a dispute, with or without the assistance of the UN. A political agreement, peace process, or diplomatic arrangement had to be in place for a UN peacekeeping mission to be mounted.[30] In short, there had to be a peace to keep, a process to facilitate, and a dialogue to support.

Established Mission Tasks. UN PKOs also came to acquire a number of general and specific functions. In general terms, peacekeeping forces could defuse tensions, stabilize a situation, and prevent the outbreak or spread of violent incidents. They could reduce anxiety, fear, and rumour, and permit the return of at least a semblance of normal conditions. Peacekeeping forces also acquired a number of specific functions. Observer missions could supervise withdrawals and detect ceasefire violations and breaches of negotiated agreements. They could act as arbiters and mediators in the case of disputes about implementation of a negotiated agreement. Interpositionary forces acted as buffers between hostile factions, to prevent outbreaks of violence. Peacekeeping contingents could also act as instruments of law and order in the absence of local authority. Finally, peacekeeping missions performed a wide variety of humanitarian tasks, from delivering relief supplies to repairing infrastructure.

Composed Primarily of Military Personnel. UN PKOs were carried out primarily by people with military status, mainly soldiers but also naval and air personnel. These personnel were disciplined and trained, responsible to their commanders, and mobile and readily available, by comparison with civilian alternatives. They could also communicate effectively with local military personnel. For the most part, peacekeepers were trained soldiers first and foremost, and the prevailing wisdom has long asserted that the best peacekeeper is a trained soldier, although the debate about specialized training for peacekeeping is a recurring one.

Proper Authority. Consistent with just war theory and international law, UN peacekeeping forces had to be despatched by the correct authorizing agency. For the most part, this has been the Security Council, although many earlier missions were authorized through the General Assembly. The mandate set by the Security Council was the foundation for the legal and operational boundaries of a mission and could not be altered without authorization from the Security Council. In the field, the mission tasks and rules of engagement (ROEs) under which peacekeepers operated flowed from the mandate, and UN peacekeeping forces were therefore under the operational control of the UN.

Reliance on Member States. As the UN has no army or force of its own, peacekeeping operations depend on the commitment and contributions — including finances, equipment, logistics support and troops — of member states to a peacekeeping mission. At the inception of a new mission, the UN calls on member states to contribute, and the mission is formed on an ad hoc basis out of whatever contributions are made. Often, contributions were smaller than what was required or lacking in capability or quality. As a result, operations were forced to improvise, with inevitable effects on the conduct of the mission.

Small States as Troop Contributors. The composition of UN peacekeeping missions also acquired a certain quality. The contingents making up UN peacekeeping forces were drawn primarily from non-great power states. During the Cold War, the superpowers and the other P5 members were seldom troop contributors. The superpowers (and often the great powers) were seen to have global interests in many regional conflicts, which clashed with the spirit of impartiality. Their involvement, therefore, was unacceptable to the parties concerned. However, the idea that UN contingents were drawn primarily from non-aligned states is a myth. In fact, many troop contributors are anything but non-aligned, as many members of NATO, for example, are troop contributors to traditional peacekeeping missions. Rather, it was the fact that participating states had no regional interests and tended to be small states with no global agenda that made them acceptable.

Non-Territorial. In another significant departure from traditional military operations, traditional peacekeeping operations did not attempt to seize or establish control over territory. UN contingents did not 'occupy' territory *against* an opponent or group of opponents; rather, it occupied territory *for* the parties to facilitate the conflict management process. To the extent that an interpositionary mission was 'territorial', it involved the patrolling or observation of an agreed zone or line negotiated with the parties to a conflict before deployment. UN contingents had no legal claim to the possession of such territory and no sovereignty over it.

CHAPTER SUMMARY

1. The original collective security mission of the United Nations was rendered impotent by the great power divisions of the Cold War in the Security Council.
2. UN peacekeeping, not mentioned in the UN Charter and developed as an ad hoc, improvised function, emerged as the UN's primary contribution to international peace and security.
3. UN peacekeeping fell in between Chapter VI (peaceful resolution of disputes) and Chapter VII (enforcement measures). Peacekeeping was therefore referred to as a "Chapter Six-and-a-half" operation.
4. UN peacekeeping evolved under two general constraints: the realities of the UN system (Cold War politics and the sovereignty protection accorded the state in the Charter) and the nature of international

conflict during the Cold War (between states or colonial powers and aspiring states).
5. Accordingly, 'traditional' peacekeeping operations acquired a distinct set of conventions born out of the UN and the Cold War world. In one prominent case where these conventions were not followed (the Congo), near-disaster ensued, which served to reinforce the limitations and boundaries of peacekeeping operations.
7. The conventions of traditional peacekeeping were as follows:

- The peacekeeping mission was impartial.
- Contingents were non-hostile and lightly armed.
- The consent of the parties to a conflict was required for deployment.
- Peacekeeping missions could not create the conditions for success.
- Peacekeepers performed certain general and specific tasks.
- They were composed primarily of military personnel.
- Missions were despatched under the authority and operational control of the UN.
- The UN relied on member states for contributions.
- Contributors tended to be smaller states.
- Peacekeeping missions were non-territorial in nature.

Chronological List of Peacekeeping Missions

June 1948 to date	UNTSO, United Nations Truce Supervision Organisation
January 1949 to date	UNMOGIP, United Nations Military Observer Group in India and Pakistan
November 1956-June 1967	UNEF I, First United Nations Emergency Force
June 1958-December 1958	UNOGIL, United Nations Observer Group in Lebanon
July 1960-June 1964	ONUC, United Nations Operation in the Congo
October 1962-April 1963	UNSF, United Nations Security Force in West New Guinea
July 1963-September 1964	UNYOM, United Nations Yemen Observer Mission
March 1964 to date	UNFICYP, United Nations Peace-keeping Force in Cyprus
May 1965-October 1966	DOMREP, Mission of the Representative of the Secretary-General in the Dominican Republic
September 1965-March 1966	UNIPOM, United Nations India-Pakistan Observation Mission
October 1973-July 1979	UNEF II, Second United Nations Emergence Force
June 1974 to date	UNDOF, United Nations Disengagement Observer Force
March 1978 to date	UNIFIL, United Nations Interim Force in Lebanon
April 1988-March 1990	UNGOMAP, United Nations Good Offices Mission in Afghanistan and Pakistan
August 1988-February 1991	UNIIMOG, United Nations Iran-Iraq Military Observer Group
January 1989-June 1991	UNAVEM I, United Nations Angola Verification Mission I
April 1989-March 1990	UNTAG, United Nations Transition Assistance Group

23 Traditional Peacekeeping During the Cold War

November 1989-January 1992	ONUCA, United Nations Observer Group in Central America
April 1991 to date	UNIKOM, United Nations Iraq-Kuwait Observation Mission
June 1991 to date	UNAVEM II, United Nations Angola Verification Mission II
July 1991 to date	ONUSAL, United Nations Observer Mission in El Salvador
September 1991 to date	MINURSO, United Nations Mission for the Referendum in Western Sahara
October 1991-March 1992	UNAMIC, United Nations Advance Mission in Cambodia
March 1992 to date	UNPROFOR, United Nations Protection Force
March 1992 to date	UNTAC, United Nations Transitional Authority in Cambodia
April 1992-April 1993	UNOSOM I, United Nations Operation in Somalia I
December 1992 to date	ONOMOZ United Nations Operation in Mozambique
May 1993-March 1995	UNOSOM II, United Nations Operation in Somalia II
August 1993 to date	UNOMIG, UN Observer Mission in Georgia
September 1993 to date	UNMIH, UN Mission in Haiti
September 1993 to date	UNOMIL, UN Mission in Liberia
October 1993 to date	UNAMIR, UN Assistance Mission for Rwanda
December 1994 to date	UNMOT, UN Military Observer Mission in Tajikistan
March 1995 to date	UNCRO, UN Confidence Restoration Operation (Croatia)
March 1995 to date	UNPREDEP, UN Preventive Deployment (Macedonia)

CHAPTER TWO

The Changing Nature of International Conflict

WARFARE SINCE THE SECOND WORLD WAR

General Trends

Changing Conditions, Conflict Management, and Military Intervention. Warfare and military thought have had certain dominant qualities since the inception of the modern state system. While there have been exceptions, for the most part warfare was conducted among states for political ends; warfare was a tool, an instrument of statecraft, a means to protect or extend the power of the state. Conflict management instruments have developed in this context. Diplomacy, mediation and adjudication, treaties, sanctions, and international institutions have all been aimed at preventing or terminating conflict between states. The United Nations was created with the aim of preventing another conflagration of the kind that engulfed the world between 1939 and 1945. However, developments in the nature of conflict since the Second World War have posed difficulties for traditional conflict management mechanisms as well as traditional military interventions using traditional military methods (which are generally referred to as the Western way of war). Both have been largely unsuited to the shifting nature of warfare, and this has compelled a search for new conflict management mechanisms and has prompted many armed forces to adopt new methods, capabilities, and techniques.

Changes in the Nature of Warfare. Warfare continues to be frequent and devastating. Estimated casualties range from 18.2 million between 1945 and 1988 to 40 million deaths in some 250 wars since 1945, and some 42 armed conflicts were under way worldwide in 1994.[1] Virtually all these conflicts have occurred in the developing world, rather than among the most powerful states. Most of these wars have been directed against local and indigenous authorities and were aimed at altering domestic circumstance or achieving independence. Another major change in the nature of conflict has been the erosion of the central position of the state as the fundamental unit of conflict or security. Other units or groups are now increasingly crucial actors, including ethnic groups, religious groups, and political factions. Wars between states are no longer the dominant form of conflict; until 1945, 80 per cent of wars were conventional interstate wars. Since 1945, 80 per cent of wars have been intrastate, unconventional wars.[2] In addition, many internationalized wars began as domestic conflicts (e.g., Afghanistan). The proportion of non-combat casualties in wars has also risen, a trend that began in the Second World War. Between 1945 and 1988, 64 per cent of casualties were civilians; today about 90 per cent of war victims are civilians.[3]

Changes in the Style of Warfare. Conflicts in the post-Second World War world also differed in style from the wars of the eighteenth and nineteenth centuries. There were very few set-piece battles, and there was often no clear front line. For the most part, they have been conducted by irregular forces with limited logistical and infrastructure support, often with poor or uncertain command and control by political authorities, whether these political authorities were local warlords or central political figures. These wars were not fought in the stages that attended so many traditional wars (crisis, declaration of war, military campaigning, defeat, and peace terms); instead, wars have been characterized by variations in intensity, with flare-ups of armed clashes alternating with periods of relative inactivity. Techniques and weaponry have been heavily improvised. There has also been a decline (or a failure to observe) traditional or western conventions as to the etiquette or customs of warfare. Finally, there has been a breakdown in the distinction between civilians and soldiers and combatants and non-combatants, with the civilian population playing an increasing role in the political and military strategies of warring factions.

The Emergence of Low-Intensity Conflict

The Nature of War and Security in the Developing World. It has been evident for some time that much of the history and theoretical approaches used to analyze war are ill-suited to the nature of conflict in the developing world, a style of warfare referred to as low-intensity conflict. The state is a less useful or irrelevant unit of analysis in these conflicts, and explanations of conflict based on systems theories, balance of power, or state decision-making structures, all informed by the study of the patterns of European and Cold War history between great powers, are very limited as instruments for investigating and understanding these conflicts. The nature of security itself is different, for an important element of the nature of conflict in the developing world is the weakness or collapse of 'failed' states. The result is that security is bound to aims and goals at the sub-state level, where most conflict takes place. Security is thus defined by sub-state group and may include regime security (security of the power position of ruling elites), communal security (protection of ethnic or religious groups), or local security (security of a collective such as a village or a geographic region). This is not to ignore the importance of external factors, such as arms supplies, patronage, and the involvement of other countries or non-state actors.

Insurgency Warfare. Insurgency warfare developed in the domestic context of conflicts in the developing world. While often linked to the liberation theologies of left-wing political movements, the techniques and style of insurgency warfare constituted a significant departure from traditional approaches to warfare. In the conduct of insurgency warfare, political strength is more important than military strength.[4] This is rather different from traditional conceptions of warfare, which recognize the importance of political factors but tend to argue that wars are won primarily by military prowess on the battlefield. For example, in the Maoist model of the conduct of an insurgency campaign, the insurgents cannot initially match the military power of the government, so they direct their efforts to building political, social and economic structures to shift the domestic correlation of forces against the government. Efforts might also be made to extend the struggle abroad diplomatically, to undermine the enemy's international position and the will of their allies, and to gain foreign support and assistance. Military operations are restricted to harassment and assassination, but as the insurgents gain strength they begin to establish bases, control areas of the countryside, and establish their own administrative structures. Finally, only when the insurgents have gained advantage in the correlation of forces might they commit their forces to a final military offensive. A key component of insurgency warfare is the focus on the defeat of the opponent's political will rather than the defeat of the enemy's military forces. For guerilla and terrorist movements that did not follow Maoist models, two elements have been universal in the conduct of insurgency warfare: a strategic political and psychological dimension aimed at developing legitimacy and political support, and a tactical military dimension aimed at establishing control over territory and instruments of governance. Such opponents are a difficult challenge for western warfighting approaches, which emphasize military prowess as the key to success in war.

An Attempt to Adjust: Counterinsurgency Warfare. The growing frequency of insurgencies and their relevance in the context of the Cold War competition sparked the development of a new expertise in warfare, initially called 'subliminal' warfare and then referred to as counterinsurgency.[5] Counterinsurgency was a political and military approach to combatting ideologically driven insurgencies, using techniques aimed at isolating the insurgent movement from its base of support (usually the local population) and preventing them from establishing control over the countryside. Techniques included a wide range of military and social activity, some of which became brutal and repressive, including suppression of dissent and forced removal or even killing of the population. New operational tactics were devised, including search and destroy missions, and military campaigns were accompanied with political campaigns aimed at securing the loyalty of population (winning hearts and minds) through social policies such as initiating reforms to undercut support for the insurgents. Despite the prominence of several insurgency wars during the Cold War period, the ability to combat insurgencies was not considered a military priority, especially in the United States; that priority was given to central front in Europe or the central command in the Middle East or other high-intensity conflict scenarios emphasizing traditional conventional conflict. As a result, western militaries — particularly the U.S. military — were slow to develop the military expertise or the requisite fusion of political, social, and military strategy that could have been so helpful for intervention (and peacekeeping) in the internal low-intensity conflicts of the immediate post-Cold War period.[6]

THE END OF THE COLD WAR AND ETHNIC AND RELIGIOUS CONFLICTS

The End of the Cold War and Regional Security Issues

No End to History: The End of the Cold War and the Developing World. While the end of the Cold War has meant the end of global war scenarios based on the rivalry between the United States and the former Soviet Union, it has highlighted long-standing regional conflicts and sparked many others. At least 19 major wars were under way in each year of the

1989-1991 period; 29 wars were under way in 1992 and 52 in 1993. All these conflicts were in the developing world.[7] While there may be an end to conflict between political and economic systems — or more likely a hiatus — the basis for regional conflicts remains intact, including competing systems of social organization, competing regional interests, clashes of civilizations, wars/conflicts characterized by ethnic or religious factors, and scarcity in various forms. The end of the Cold War spells the end of bipolarity and ideological rivalry as the central aspect of the developed world's penetration into the developing world. This does not mean that penetration of the great powers into the developing world is no longer a concern. There are numerous concerns in the developing world with respect to military activity, humanitarian intervention, and economic penetration and dependence (often labelled neo-colonialism and/or economic imperialism).

A 'New' Third World or an 'Old' Third World? The larger context of the developing world in the post-Cold War era is one of contrasts. On balance, the end of the Cold War did not bring many positives with respect to the security situation in the developing world. Larger issues will continue to play a role in the genesis of conflict and instability in the developing world. The developing world holds 75 per cent of the world's population but accounts for only 20 per cent of the world's economic product. Half the earth's population suffers from malnutrition; 1.3 billion people live in absolute poverty; and 17 million die each year from preventable diseases. One billion adults are illiterate.[8] Science, technology, and information are controlled by one-quarter of the global population, which also consumes the vast majority of the world's energy reserves. Environmental degradation and pollution are increasingly affecting developing countries.[9] The potential for violence and conflict is high, and the capacity of developing countries to mobilize resources against this potential is inherently limited. Against this structural backdrop, the end of the Cold War has had the following consequences:

- The value or usefulness of developing countries as allies or symbols has declined, and along with it the leverage that this usefulness gave to developing countries. The non-aligned movement is also in question, as there is no longer a global rivalry to be non-aligned against.
- With the collapse of the Soviet Union, developing countries lost an alternative model of development and social organization and an anti-western patron with great political, economic, and military power.

Potential alternative patrons (China, Islamic countries) do not have the resources and tend to be selective about who they support.
- For developing countries' governments, the fading memories of decolonization will mean their own records will become increasingly important as blaming the colonial legacy fades as a convincing explanation for poor economic performance.
- The challenge to the legitimacy of colonial boundaries continues, despite efforts to overcome boundary and territorial disputes.
- Concerns about the potential for neglect of the developing world in the absence of a global strategic imperative are matched by concerns about economic penetration and control and intervention based on resource access, wars of conscience, proliferation, and global environmental and population concerns.
- There has been little or no change in the developed world's position in the international economy.
- Many developing countries are facing increased threats to their social stability from poverty, resource scarcity, migration of peoples across borders, and paralyzed political processes.

The Return of History: Ethnic and Religious Conflict After the Cold War

'New' Conflicts on the Block. The phenomenon of ethnic and religious conflict is not new; in fact it is older than state conflict. However, there has been a recent surge in the frequency and intensity of these conflicts. Between 1945 and 1981, 258 cases of ethnic violence were identified. In 1993-94, some 50 ethnic conflicts were being waged, each responsible for an average of 80,000 deaths and together creating some 27 million refugees.[10] Some of these conflicts have achieved a very high international profile. The explanations for this intensification of ethnic, nationalist, and religious conflict include the collapse of old imperial orders and decolonization, the collapse of more recent federal or imperial states (Yugoslavia and the U.S.S.R.), and the weakening of many multi-ethnic states and the collapse of failed states.

The Nature of Ethnicity. As a general definition, ethnicity is the communal identity of people who are classed together by cultural, social, and sometimes physical similarities.[11] Specifically, ethnic groups share some combination of the following:

- a name (and accompanying identity)
- a common history (common ancestry with shared memories)
- a link with a territory
- shared social customs, culture, and economy
- physical traits
- a measure of internal solidarity (group consciousness)

These qualities give a group the will and capacity for collective action. If ethnic identity is diffuse, fractured, or otherwise divided, there is very seldom the potential for organized conflict.

The Complexity of the Ethnicity Issue. As a motivation for action, ethnicity is not easily isolated and defined. Ethnicity is not a homogenous belief, felt with the same intensity among all members of a group. Ethnicity is influenced by social construction, the creation of myth and legend, and can be reinforced (intentionally or unintentionally) through schooling and social life. In addition, ethnicity can have a voluntary element, in the sense that individuals and communities have some range of choice over how much they wish to define themselves by ethnic criteria. Ethnicity, then, is not a menu or qualifying exam of items that identify a group. Rather, it is an endowment that is bestowed upon individuals, and different elements of that endowment may be more or less active in some individuals or groups when certain issues are at stake. Political or religious differences may spark conflicts that appear ethnic or acquire an ethnic dimension. Caution must therefore be exercised in using ethnicity as the explanation for violence that has an ethnic character, because the origins of violence are often interwoven with social, political, or economic elements.

Explanations and Causes of Ethnic Conflict. A number of sparks, or smouldering embers, can ignite ethnic conflict.[12] First, ethnicity can lead to conflict through the hostility of ethnic groups in close proximity. This can have a variety of origins, some or all of which may be present in any one conflict. Many of these are domestic in nature and include the following:

- Economic grievances, where the control or dominance over economic power by one group can lead to conflicts over entitlements and resources, and the right or power to control them. The conflict is therefore based

on a struggle against economic discrimination, which is often entrenched in the economic operation of a country.
- Positional interests, concerning representation and power in posts in government, the military, and the police. The conflict may then take on the shape of a struggle against the dominance of one ethnic group over the administrative and security apparatus of the state.
- Conflict over territorial rights, or the history of possession of resource assets. In such conflicts, the parties attempt to seize territory regarded as part of an historical ethnic endowment or homeland.
- Psychological or primordial factors can be central; revenge or the redress of historical grievances and racial hatreds can lead to brutal efforts (the euphemistically termed 'ethnic cleansing') aimed at the purification of society or territory by killing or forcing other groups into flight.
- Finally, ethnic conflicts can originate in incitement by leaders. Fanning resentment and opening old hostilities are often used as instruments to mobilize support and create scapegoats for economic or social hardships. Sometimes, this appeal to identity is not intended to lead to violence; at other times, there is a conscious effort to direct ethnic impulses toward violent actions.

A second explanation for ethnic conflicts is that national, regional, and international forces are too weak to maintain order, well-being, and the security of individual groups. When empires break up, the human geography of a territory often looks like a patchwork of peoples, with islands and enclaves of one group often surrounded by another. In such environments, 'security dilemmas' can develop between peoples as they have developed among states; other groups come to be seen as potential threats, and attempts to protect group security are interpreted as hostile acts by neighbours, starting (or renewing) a cycle of mistrust and hostility. Specifically, arming for the defence of a group can be interpreted by other groups as preparation for offensive action.

Third, ethnic conflicts may originate in the clash between the state and ethnicity. The nation state is built on an internal tension between the sovereignty of the state based on territorial demarcation and the imposition of this sovereignty on the ethnic, cultural, and religious divisions of the world. Only 10 per cent of the more than 170 states in the world can be characterized as ethnically homogenous. One study identifies 233 significant minority groups that are present in 93 different countries.[13] However, state nationalism is built around loyalty to the state, and if this is challenged by loyalty to ethnic nationalism, conflict can erupt. Ethnic conflict can also be created by the disjuncture between ethnicity and nationalism. State-based nationalism and ethnic-based nationalism often clash: state nationalism tends to be inclusive within a state's borders, while ethnic nationalism tends to be exclusive. Ethnic nationalism may undermine the state by claiming autonomy or separation for an ethnic group or unification with members of the group living outside state boundaries (a phenomenon known as irredentism).

Explanations for the Intensity of Ethnic Conflict. Ethnic conflicts tend to be fierce and brutal, largely because of the psychological dimensions of ethnicity. The basis of ethnic conflicts lie in primordial elements of self-identification and self-preservation. One of the characteristics of ethnic conflicts is the close connection between the civilian and the combatant, with civilians often being an intended or direct target of attack. This is the case for the following reasons:

- Civilians are the centre of group power, the source of soldiers and food and support. As a result, they are attacked to weaken the military and political potential of other groups.
- Civilians are symbols of the group identity of an opponent and as such are subject to demonization and dehumanization as representatives of an evil, poisonous or insidious presence.
- Civilians are subject to revenge atrocities, committed as retribution for past grievances in previous outbreaks of violence between ethnic groups.
- The 'low-tech' nature of ethnic warfare, and the predominance of light weapons as the instruments of such conflicts, means that soft targets are the most viable.
- Ethnic groups are often intermingled. The early stages of ethnic conflicts tend to involve securing and taking areas held by other groups, and battle lines are often defined by demographic boundaries.
- Territorial gain is reflected in the composition of people living in a defined region. Forcing populations to leave is therefore a cornerstone of military campaigns designed to make territorial gains.

Spillover and the Refugee Dimension. The general refugee crisis of some 44 million refugees includes huge numbers fleeing regional conflicts. In 1993, an estimated 18.5 million refugees worldwide were fleeing the dangers and ravages of war.[14] The problem of refugee flows created by conflict in general and ethnic conflict in particular (again, because of the importance of the civilian population in ethnic clashes) not only poses tremendous humanitarian challenges but can contribute to the widening of ethnic conflicts in several respects. The offer of sanctuary (or refusing it) can drag neighbouring countries into conflict. Refugee populations and camps can serve as bases for fighters. The costs and demands on the resources of host states can create regional friction, as can policies of forced repatriation, and the presence of large numbers of refugees can threaten the cultural identity of host states.

Religious Conflict. Religious conflicts have a genesis all their own, although religious conflicts are often intertwined with ethnic conflicts or are a component of an ethnic conflict. In addition, religion can intensify conflicts with origins in other factors. The dynamics of religious conflict are similar to those of ethnic conflict and include the following:

- Religious conflict can break out between religious groups with different views.
- Conflict can break out over the position or status of religions within a state and can include such concerns as representation in government and administration, religious rights, freedom from persecution, and separatist sentiments of those seeking union with the territory of religious brethren in neighbouring countries.
- The link between religion and territory can result in competing land claims.
- Extremist or fundamentalist individuals or groups can act as a catalyst for violence. Religious fundamentalism (intolerant and dogmatic religious literalism) can spark wider hostilities, and violence can be used as a tactic by extremist groups.
- Religion can sanction killing. This can be done directly, where religious leaders call for violence, or religion can be used to justify violence by individuals or groups.
- Religion and the secular state can collide. At issue is the organization of society and authority in society, and whether this should be controlled by political principles or religious principles. This is complicated by the fact that religious organizations are often as effective or more effective as centres of community life, providers of services, and providers of leadership.

Factional or Intra-ethnic Conflict. In some cases, intrastate conflicts are neither ethnic nor religious in nature. Instead, conflict occurs between peoples with common ethnic roots, religion, language and social customs. Such conflicts are therefore factional or 'intra-ethnic' in character; the divisions between the participants are based on political, family, or clan cleavages. Such divisions can be extremely deep; as a result, factional intra-ethnic conflicts can take on many of the characteristics of ethnic conflicts and may in fact be indistinguishable from them to someone unfamiliar with the society or country. The dynamics of factional wars include:

- conflict over the control of the apparatus of the government and the state;
- conflict over positional interests, representation and rights;
- conflict over territorial and resource claims;
- conflict over economic grievances and discrimination; and
- the convergence of political actors (parties, local governments, and state bureaucracies) and factions.

The Challenge for Intervention, Management, and Conflict Prevention

Intervention in Ethnic and Religious Conflicts: General Obstacles. The nature of ethnic and religious conflicts makes them resistant to traditional methods of management and termination, a result of what James B. Seaton has called the "de-Westernization" of war.[15] As a result, argues J.M. Beach, Western militaries (and, it might be added, their political masters and the public) find these wars "uncomfortable", because they are inconsistent with the principles of the "western way of war".[16] This discomfort stems from both larger political and operational challenges:

- State diplomacy has limited relevance in such conflicts, which take place within states and in contexts where the state mechanisms have collapsed or are irrelevant.
- The intensity of such conflicts, and the commitment of the warring factions to the defence of their core values and even their existence, is such that negotiation, mediation and compromise are often difficult to achieve.
- Information and intelligence on the aims of the antagonists are often lacking or are speculative.
- As many of the potential solutions or management methods involve changes to the internal apparatus of a state, the obstacles inherent in any involvement in internal state affairs inevitably present themselves.

- Furthermore, because these conflicts are rooted in social history, an understanding of the conflict, the parties and personalities involved, and of what conflict management techniques might be applicable, must be built from the ground up in each new case of ethnic and religious conflict.
- Western military establishments must move toward enhancing their understanding of the political, social, cultural, and psychological aspects of conflict if they are to be successful instruments of intervention or conflict management in these conflicts.[17]

Intervention in Ethnic and Religious Conflicts: Operational Obstacles. In addition to the general difficulties confronting intervention in ethnic and religious conflicts, significant operational difficulties face intervention forces and their efforts to terminate or manage hostilities:

- Warring groups do not reflect the same organization or characteristics of states, or western model political establishments or armed forces. The force of the warring factions does not represent the state, but rather a faction, group, or individual within it.
- Because of this, the interests and objectives of these factions may be difficult to discern. Rather than fighting for a state's "national interests", they will fight for ethnic, group, territorial, or even individual interests.
- It is difficult to distinguish between the general population and the combatants, which are often one and the same. The population can also provide a shield or an escape and camouflage medium for warring factions. Interventions will take place in "complex human environments", as control of the population is often a key objective. This makes the struggle for the allegiance of the population and the instruments of this struggle — image, public relations, information dissemination — of critical importance to all sides, including peacekeeping contingents.[18]
- A conflict will be over control of the population, not just territory (indeed, increasingly the two will be intimately linked in concepts of control).[19] Therefore, intervention efforts will have to move beyond pure territorial objectives or settlements and must consider human objectives and demographics.
- Intervention efforts will include missions that will assist and co-operate, and fight and oppose the same group simultaneously.
- There will not always be a clearly defined enemy. Rather, there will be gradations between the various warring parties with respect to their status as supporters or opponents of peacekeeping or intervention forces.

These may change, and sub-factions within warring parties may hold different positions and relationships with intervention forces.
- In cases where a clearly defined enemy does exist, that enemy will not operate according to traditional western modes of conventional combat but will pursue insurgency tactics designed to neutralize their technological and firepower disadvantages.
- The application of military force, especially firepower, has limited utility in addressing complex socio-political-military problems.
- Heavy demands will be placed on small-unit manoeuvre and the quality of personnel, particularly junior commanders:

The reality of uncomfortable conflict is that the units are often small, sometimes covert, with the distinction between them and the surrounding civilians being blurred at best. Command is de-centralized, with junior commanders making what can often be operational level decisions, such as the detaining of opposing leaders, or opening fire on crowds of rioters, without reference to higher command. Attempts by high command to micro-manage such situations by restricting actions can lead to further problems caused by frustration.[20]

- The objectives of intervention forces will be different from those characteristic of traditional military campaigns. Objectives will be less clearly defined in the sense that they will focus less on territorial gain, seizing cities and destroying the opponent's capacity to fight, and will focus more on pacification, policing, and restoring "normality".
- Success will be less easy to measure, not only because objectives are less quantifiable, but because success will be determined in large part by social and political developments.
- Interventions will also be long-term propositions, because of the importance of larger social and developmental factors, the attrition nature of insurgency-style conflicts, and the resistance of ethnic and religious conflicts to political machinations such as treaties and ceasefires. This has implications for the political will of sponsoring organizations and contributing countries and increases the importance of logistics and sustainability.

The ability of western military establishments (and, just as important, their political masters) to meet these general and operational challenges will depend on the effectiveness of efforts to overcome traditional modes of thinking, bureaucratic inertia, and the self-isolation of militaries — the so-called "fortress cloister".[21]

Conflict Prevention: Some Proposed Strategies. In light of the perceived failure of traditional conflict management and intervention instruments in ethnic and religious conflicts, some proposals have sought to move beyond tradition. However, these proposals are fraught with obstacles and possible negative consequences.

- Prevention through Early Warning. In keeping with the general philosophy that an ounce of prevention is worth a pound of cure, the aim of conflict prevention is to try to prevent, minimize or contain non-violent disputes before they spiral out of control into violent clashes. Early warning and a record of historically significant indicators are vital to the success of this instrument. Warning signs include persistent cleavages between ethnic groups; a history of suppression; elite use of authority to maintain an ethnic group's power or position in society; a society that is unstable or exhausted by political or natural disaster; and the presence of a mythology of exclusion and inferiority. The problem with conflict prevention strategies is that they presuppose a high level of external co-ordination and agreement, not only on the criteria for intervention but also on the commitment and will to follow through with it.
- Moderating the Organizing Principle of the State. If the state is part of the problem, another mechanism to defuse or pre-empt ethnic or religious disputes is to give such groups greater autonomy. One option would be to increase the rights of such groups within states, by granting them rights and privileges and some degree of autonomy. Another option is to recognize a form of dual sovereignty, such that state and ethno/religious modes of organization and loyalties co-exist. State borders could be revised along ethnic lines. A final and ambitious option would be a move toward a world based on ethnic territoriality. These options raise as many questions as they answer, however: how do we move from a state-centred world to a new form of organization? How viable would a world of ethno/religious units be? How could other cleavages (e.g., economic) be accommodated? How can states be persuaded to make concessions to ethno/religious groups? Are societies based on multiple sovereignties viable? Would reopening border issues lead to even more conflict?
- A social process approach. If the key to avoiding conflicts in the future is behaviour modification, then education is the long-term answer. The problem of ethnic and religious conflict must be addressed at the level of the individual, through individual education. In this way, conflict,

ethnic hatreds and suspicions, and the cycle of violence can be neutralized from below, as opposed to from above through political leaders. Of course, this process is slow, even if we accept that perceptions can be altered in such a fashion.

THE FUTURE OF ARMED CONFLICT

Post-Industrial Warfare/Industrial Warfare

A Fourth Generation of War? Earlier generations of warfare were characterized by innovations in massed manpower, massed firepower, and manoeuvre. Developments in society (the citizen army, nationalism) and technology (from iron to the nuclear bomb) influenced the development of warfare and vice versa. Based on changes in these eternal influences on the character of warfare, a fourth generation of war may be emerging. The factors that are changing the shape of warfare are many and varied and include:

- a political scene characterized by more actors on the world stage;
- an economic scene characterized by greater interdependence;
- a social scene characterized by the development of international networks, linked by various types of communication media that are increasingly interconnected and increasingly outside government control;
- the continued development and diffusion of technologies of miniaturization, data storage and transfer, chemistry and biology, and autonomous systems and robotics; and
- the increased importance of information and knowledge as factors in political and economic success.

This fourth generation of warfare will see an increasing shift toward emphasis on the political factors in conflicts. As conflicts become more based on social, ethnic, religious, cultural, and other schisms, political acumen will become more important as an element of success. In addition, many of these conflicts will not involve high-intensity combat on the battlefield but will rely instead on political manoeuvre, information and disinformation, and focused acts of violence for political/media purposes as decisive elements in the outcome of a struggle. This phenomenon is not new, but these factors will become increasingly important in future conflicts. Nor does this mean that Clauswitzian warfare is dead; it means that this kind of warfare will become increasingly rare. As J.M.

Beach has argued, "uncomfortable conflicts can be played out more on the political/media stage than on the battlefield."[22]

The Importance of Knowledge and Information. Fourth generation warfare will also see the emergence of information, together with control and dissemination of information and disinformation, as decisive factors in success. Knowledge and information will become increasingly important force multipliers, and the arenas in which this information warfare will take place will include a wide variety of local, domestic, and international venues. The media and public opinion will be key arenas. As a whole, this element of conflict can be described as 'netwar' — information warfare at the grand level between societies or states or those that control them.[23] The nature of netwar includes the following features:

- efforts to disrupt, damage, or change what a society thinks about itself and the world around it;
- a focus on elite or public opinion (or both);
- conducted by psywar operations, propaganda, political and cultural subversion, deception, interference and manipulation of the media, infiltration of computer networks and databases, and foment of dissident movements across social networks in a society or country.

Again, the phenomenon is not new. What is new is the increased importance of this dimension of warfare, as well as the new media and technologies now available for exploiting it. Fourth generation warfare will not necessarily be high-technology, high-intensity warfare, but may be extremely complex low-intensity warfare, which will have qualities not unlike a more complex version of insurgency warfare.

Future Challenges for Conflict Prevention and Management

The Importance of Knowledge and Information. The increasing emphasis on the political dimensions of a conflict, its social, cultural, and ethno/religious roots, and the importance of information and the media create new challenges for conflict management in general and peacekeeping or humanitarian intervention in particular. Knowledge and information will be increasingly important determinants of success in conflict management operations. If peacekeeping or interventionary forces are not well-informed about the ethnic, religious, cultural, and social environment in which they must act, their capacity to understand the motives, objectives, and actions of local factions or groups will be severely hampered; this in turn will weaken the capacity of peacekeepers to negotiate with or compel action by parties to local ceasefires or national reconciliation agreements. Peacekeepers must know which buttons to press in certain situations, and they cannot obtain this knowledge without an understanding of the environment in which they operate. This will likely change the content of peacekeeping or interventionary forces to some extent. A greater civilian component, composed of experts, expatriots, and police personnel, will be increasingly relevant to mission priorities.

Conflict Management and Information Capabilities. Future peacekeeping and interventionary forces will be heavily engaged in an information battle. This battle will take place in three arenas: within the country where the peacekeeping or interventionary force is deployed; in the domestic setting (both public and elite opinion) of countries contributing to the peacekeeping or interventionary force; and in the arena of world opinion. In country or in theatre, peacekeeping forces will require an enhanced information capability. This should include a radio station capability, production of a newsletter (for environments where literacy rates are high), and a mandate to seize or destroy media outlets controlled by hostile factions that are being used to incite violence. The need to combat propaganda, misinformation, and rumour is a crucial aspect of the pacification or peace mission. The importance of the domestic information environment (within contributing countries) is also crucial. A skilful opponent can attempt to manipulate domestic opinion to constrain or even terminate a country's involvement in a peacekeeping mission. Alternatively, an opponent can target elite opinion to achieve the same objective. To combat this, peacekeeping countries must be able to explain their involvement in a given mission and counteract negative media images. Finally, the same battle against propaganda and disinformation will have to be fought at the international level. The development of an information capability at the United Nations would be a start toward a capacity to counteract information gathered by international media and second or third sources.

The Demands of Information Warfare on Peacekeeping and Intervention Forces. Technology will continue to increase in importance as a factor in the success of peacekeeping and interventionary missions, but the application of technology will likely change somewhat. Instead of using superior firepower technology, peacekeeping and intervention forces will be making greater use of information technologies. However, this will place added strain on one of the already problematic schisms in most peacekeeping missions — wide discrepancies in the training, equipment, and technical capacity of peacekeeping units. Increased demands for technically sophisticated and informed contingents will be placed on contributing countries, which will often lack these capabilities. This raises the question of whether some peacekeeping countries ought to begin to specialize in this increasingly important capacity.

Difficulties of Conducting Information Warfare. Application and management of the information dimension of interventionary efforts will be both difficult and demanding. The record of psychological or information warfare is not one of robust effectiveness, even for countries with a relatively high level of capability and expertise: witness the experience of the United States in Vietnam, Grenada, and El Salvador and of Great Britain in Cyprus, Kenya, Aden, and Northern Ireland. Co-ordinating such operations in a UN context will pose yet another set of challenges. Seizing radio or media outlets could provoke a backlash and the development of underground capabilities, which are difficult to silence. Information management and manipulation must be carefully blended with transparency and candidness, to promote legitimacy rather than create suspicion.

New and Emerging Threats. UN contingents will encounter a growing number of potential threats to their personnel. On one side of the threat spectrum, UN personnel will be subject to attack or the threat of attack from a wider range of weapons systems. As more sophisticated arms continue to proliferate, more and more warring parties will have access to stand-off weapons systems, anti-armour systems, long-range mortars and artillery, and more sophisticated small arms. Attacks on UN installations or personnel with truck or car bombs are also a danger. In addition, UN peacekeeping personnel may be subject to attacks by weapons of mass destruction in the future. Such attacks could include gas and biological warfare agents released through sophisticated or crude delivery systems, introduced into local water supplies, or even left by hand (as in the Tokyo subway attacks). On the other side of the threat spectrum, UN peacekeeping personnel may come under increasing threat from rioters, looters, or bandits, as well as desperate locals seeking anything of value. UN peacekeeping personnel may also be threatened increasingly with detainment and used as hostages, or targeted in efforts to undercut public support in contributing countries. Another potential threat is that warring factions opposed to the UN's presence may not be content to attack peace-keeping personnel.

Contributing countries may be subject to attack by individuals, groups, or agents of states or sub-state factions opposed to UN involvement. These attacks may take comparatively mild forms, such as vandalism, or more serious forms, such as terrorist attacks or assassination attempts. Taking the fight to contributing countries would be aimed at undercutting domestic support for a country's contribution to a given mission. Of course, all these threats are closely linked to the nature of UN involvement in a country. If the UN is welcome under traditional peacekeeping precepts, these threats are unlikely to emerge. If the UN is not welcome, and is opposed by hostile factions that regard the UN and its contingents as opponents, these threats will be increasingly likely to materialize.

CHAPTER SUMMARY

1. The nature of international conflict has been evolving away from warfare between states for purposes of conquest, territorial gain, or political advantage and toward conflict between sub-state groups, including national liberation and separatist movements, ethnic and religious groups, and local factions.
2. The style of warfare has also changed, from the prevalence of high-intensity conflict, characterized by the fighting and preparation for total war, to low-intensity conflict and insurgency warfare, characterized by small unit operations, a political emphasis, and prolonged struggle.
3. The end of the Cold War offers little hope for the emergence of larger structural constraints on the emergence of conflict in the developing world. Most of the underlying causes of such conflicts — weak states, poverty, territorial and resource disputes, and historical animosities — remain in place.
4. The complex nature of ethnicity, together with the intensity of emotion and commitment to identity, makes ethnic (and religious) conflicts particularly intense, harmful to civilians, and resistant to conflict management efforts, which face enormous political and operational obstacles.
5. Knowledge and information about the history, culture, and social setting of a conflict will be increasingly important as a force multiplier and as a factor in successful conflict management.

6. In the future, the emergence of a 'fourth generation' of warfare will present additional challenges to conflict management efforts. Increasingly, conflicts will also be played out in the political and information arena, for influence over local opinion, domestic opinion in contributing countries, and international opinion. Conflict management efforts must acquire an 'information war' capability, to challenge disinformation and propaganda aimed at disrupting their efforts.
7. New threats to UN personnel and contributing countries will emerge, widening the threat spectrum faced by peacekeeping and especially peacemaking operations:

- UN peacekeeping personnel can expect to encounter an increasing variety of weapons systems of increasing sophistication. Weapons are easily accessible on international arms markets, both open and covert. The manufacturing capabilities of many countries in the small arms and support weapons fields are increasing, widening the potential supplier base.
- UN peacekeeping personnel may be subject to attacks by weapons of mass destruction in the future. Such attacks could include gas and biological warfare agents. They could be delivered by sophisticated or crude delivery systems, introduced into local water supplies, or even left by hand (as in the Tokyo subway attacks).
- UN peacekeeping personnel may come under increasing threat from rioters, looters, or bandits, as well as desperate locals seeking anything of value.
- UN peacekeeping personnel may be increasingly threatened with detainment and used as hostages, or targeted to undercut public support in contributing countries.
- Contributing countries may be subject to attack by individuals, groups, or agents of states or sub-state factions opposed to UN involvement. These attacks may take comparatively mild forms, such as vandalism, or more serious forms, such as terrorist attacks or assassination attempts.
- UN peacekeeping personnel and contributing countries will encounter the information dimension of warfare with greater frequency. This will take the form of the local spread of disinformation and propaganda directed against UN personnel and similar campaigns mounted against the leadership and public of contributing countries.

CHAPTER THREE

The Changing Nature of Peacekeeping

THE TRANSITION FROM COLD WAR TO POST-COLD WAR

The New International Environment: The Role of the UN at Fifty

The Post-Cold War Environment and the UN Agenda. The end of the Cold War removed the dominant global strategic division that characterized and influenced almost every aspect of international life for more than 40 years. In its absence, a variety of global issues have risen in prominence and have presented new challenges to a United Nations that is still adapting to the absence of the Cold War superpower rift. These issues include outbreaks of nationalist, ethnic, and religious conflict at the substate level; political fragmentation; the proliferation of weapons of mass destruction; ecological and demographic problems; refugees (in 1970, UNHCR processed some 2.5 million refugees; in 1993, it processed more than 18 million); and international agreements on arms control, resource use, transportation, communication, and space.[1] The UN is therefore confronted with a very broad agenda after the Cold War, an agenda that includes both security issues and issues of the global commons, economic development, and international regulation.

The UN and International Peace and Security After the Cold War. For supporters of the United Nations, the post-Cold War environment was supposed to be an historic opportunity, a chance for the United Nations to act as an agent of global and regional conflict management in the way envisioned by its creators. These high expectations have been largely disappointed, and they have been disappointed in no small part because of the problems afflicting UN peacekeeping missions. In particular, the very high profile of the UN's troubles in Somalia and the former Yugoslavia have discredited the UN in the eyes of many. John Ruggie, for example, has accused the UN of outright strategic failure in its efforts to manage regional conflicts after the Cold War.[2] Newspaper reports and television accounts reveal almost daily examples of UN impotence in the face of brutal violence and human rights abuses. The impact of this coverage on elite and public perception of the UN should not be underestimated. While many UN missions of lesser profile have had a measure of success, the UN as a whole is losing credibility as an effective instrument for action in the security realm.

The Future of International Institutions: Eroding or Adapting? This raises the question of the future of the United Nations in the post-Cold War world. The future of international institutions has been a matter of intense theoretical debate, now that the superpower overlay is no longer present.[3] 'Neo-realists' argue that existing international institutions — including the UN — reflected the distribution of power and the existence of a global threat during the Cold War. With the shift in that distribution of power and the collapse of the threat, neo-realists are sceptical that international institutions can develop or even survive beyond the conditions that prompted their formation.[4] For 'neo-liberals', institutions can survive and adapt, because states have learned the value of co-operation and will seek to preserve it. For neo-realists, institutions are not particularly meaningful. There is little evidence to suggest that multilateral frameworks and institutions significantly affect the behaviour of states in an anarchic, self-help environment. For neo-liberals, the preservation or development of regional co-operation, especially multilateral co-operation and institutions, is regarded as a bulwark against increasing tensions, conflict, and warfare. Multilateralism means peace and stability, or at least a good shot at it. The question for the UN, especially in light of the troubles it has experienced, is whether it will fall into disrepair and disrepute, and whether it will or can have a defining role in the international system after the Cold War.

UN Reform and Peacekeeping

UN Reform and the Security Council, Representation, and Administration. As an institution the United Nations has also been assailed by critics who argue it is in sore need of reform to reflect new realities.[5] Prominent criticisms are directed at the Security Council.[6] The Security Council reflects the post-Second World War situation, the permanent five (P5) are all nuclear weapons states, and Japan and Germany are not represented despite their economic power. The pattern of representation at the UN has also been criticized, particularly by developing countries. They charge that the developing world is underrepresented, not only in the Security Council but in all UN bodies, and that the west has disproportionate control over all components of UN operations. Suggestions for reform include widening the membership of the Security Council, giving it a more 'representative' character, abolishing the veto, or giving every continent a veto in some form. The administrative structure of the UN has also been the subject of attacks, primarily from developed countries. From this perspective, the UN is a bureaucratic nightmare: it wastes money, its agencies fight one another, and it is staffed by too many lazy, uncaring, or incompetent individuals. The UN is organized into too many administrative structures that are run like little fiefdoms. Administrative reform is aimed at streamlining UN structures and making UN officials more accountable and responsible.

UN Reform and Peacekeeping. Peacekeeping reform has also been the subject of intense scrutiny.[7] The UN has been engaged in efforts to improve its capacity to mount, maintain, and control peacekeeping missions. The Department of Peacekeeping Operations (DPKO) has created a 24-hour Situation Centre to provide a monitoring and response function at UN Headquarters. A Conceptual Planning Unit and a Generic Planning Unit have also been created, with responsibility for specific regional contingency planning and the development of standardized mission templates respectively. Both units are under the Mission Planning Service (MPS), which has overall responsibility for contingency planning. In 1992 the Department of Humanitarian Affairs initiated development of a Humanitarian Early Warning System (HEWS). In 1993 a Standby Forces Planning Team was formed to establish standby arrangements with member states, to create a standby roster of forces and capabilities available to the UN, and to decrease the response time of member states with respect to UN requests for contributions. An equipment stockpile was also established at Brindisi, Italy. While these measures are laudable, they have limitations. The 24-hour Situation Centre, while a vast improvement over having no such capability at all, is still understaffed and has only the rudimentary capabilities required to exercise its functions, with little depth to perform broader planning or preparatory tasks. The MPS is also short-staffed, as is the Standby Arrangements Team. The standby arrangements system has not been a great success, as member states have been reluctant to offer information. The standby arrangements roster thus lacks depth. Finally, the equipment stockpile at Brindisi is expensive to maintain, and much of the equipment is old or in need of extensive maintenance. In addition, peacekeeping operations suffer from the following shortcomings:

- limited logistical capabilities available to the Secretariat (DPKO);
- poor communications between UN HQ and field missions, and poor information and intelligence capabilities;
- an inefficient command and control system in the field;
- no overall 'information' capability;
- slow mission start-up, requiring an improvement in the UN's ability to react rapidly in crisis.[8] The existing process, involving Security Council authority, submission of financial budget information to the Fifth Committee for approval, requests to member states for contributions, and transport of personnel and equipment, results in four- to nine-month reaction times. In Cambodia, an agreement was signed on the ground in September 1991, but it was six months until the first units of UNTAC began to arrive in March 1992;
- inadequate performance of troops from non-traditional donors;
- lack of strategic sea and airlift;
- lack of tactical mobility (especially by air).

Agenda for Peace and the Terminological Swamp. Just as the term peacekeeping has no generally accepted definition, the use of terms with respect to the UN role in peace and security has been plagued with definitional uncertainty. In June 1992, Secretary-General Boutros Boutros-Ghali published a document called *Agenda for Peace*, in which he proposed to enhance the role of the UN in international peace and security and suggested the following structure of mission descriptions and definitions:

- Preventive diplomacy — action to prevent disputes from arising between parties, to prevent existing disputes from escalating into conflicts and limit the spread of the latter when they occur.
- Peacemaking — action to bring hostile parties to an agreement, essentially through such peaceful means as those foreseen in Chapter VI of the Charter of the United Nations.
- Peacekeeping — deployment of a United Nations presence in the field, hitherto with the consent of all the parties concerned. Peacekeeping is a technique that expands the possibilities for both the prevention of conflict and the making of peace.
- Peacebuilding — action to identify and support structures that will tend to strengthen and solidify peace in order to prevent a relapse into conflict.

Unfortunately, these descriptions did not clarify matters. There was widespread dissatisfaction with the Secretary-General's terminology, because the boundaries between the terms were vague and imprecise. In addition, the term 'peacemaking' was often used to describe enforcement actions or more forceful peacekeeping operations.[9] In the absence of clear definitions, the number of terms in use proliferated to include peacemaking, second generation peacekeeping, peace enforcement, peace restoring, stability operations, extended peacekeeping, aggravated peacekeeping, peacekeeping with muscle, peacekeeping with teeth, and robust peacekeeping, among others.[10] This struggle with definitions reflected the conceptual uncertainties surrounding the changing nature of peacekeeping operations. In addition, the terms used had to reflect at least in part the legal context of the operation, the mandate and aim of the operation, and the nature of the forces involved. In short, defining terms was difficult. This study uses the following terminological system:

- Traditional Peacekeeping Operations are operations authorized without invoking Chapter VII in response to requests for UN assistance in interstate or intrastate conflicts. These involve military and civilian operations aimed at facilitating the implementation and maintenance of a cessation of hostilities through the use of observers, interpositionary forces and/or national reconciliation and reconstruction efforts. The parties involved consent to the operation. Examples include UNFICYP, UNOMIG, and UNAVEM.[11]
- Peace Enforcement Operations are operations authorized under Chapter VII of the UN Charter in response to humanitarian crises or civil war within a state. These involve military and civilian operations in an intrastate setting, aimed at creating the conditions required for successful humanitarian relief operations and national reconciliation and reconstruction efforts. The consent of all the parties to all the provisions of the mandate is absent or incomplete. Examples include UN operations such as UNPROFOR and UNOSOM II, as well as UN-authorized operations such as UNITAF and I-FOR.
- Collective Security Enforcement Operations are operations authorized under Chapter VII of the UN Charter in response to external aggression by a state. These involve war operations in an interstate setting, aimed at achieving military victory and the restoration of the *status quo ante*. The consent of the aggressor state is absent. The Korean War and the Gulf War are the only two examples of this form of operation.

This study uses the term peace enforcement operations to refer to operations that are qualitatively distinct from traditional peacekeeping operations. When reference is made to all operations under UN auspices, this study uses the term UN peace operations.

THE CHANGING NATURE OF PEACEKEEPING MISSIONS

The Qualities of Second Generation Peacekeeping

Peacekeeping in Flux. Post-Cold War peacekeeping efforts are undergoing fundamental change in nature and scope.[12] The enterprise of peacekeeping as it developed during the Cold War is now caught between an international agenda that places nationalist, ethnic and religious conflict and human rights among its highest security priorities, and the problems associated with international involvement and intervention in such disputes. Traditional peacekeeping precepts, with their firmly established principles of political and operational conduct, have at least momentarily been forsaken in many UN operations. Now favoured is a more aggressive and intrusive approach, an innovation deemed necessary in response to ethnic and civil strife in the international system after the Cold War. This approach has fallen in a grey zone between Chapter Six-and-a-half operations and Chapter VII operations. The conduct of this new style of UN mission differs fundamentally from the conventions that evolved from traditional peacekeeping operations during the Cold War. This section highlights the nature of these differences.

Conducted Within States. For the most part, new peacekeeping missions have been conducted within the borders of states, rather than between them. Of the 11 new operations created since January 1992, all but two have involved deployment within a country in cases of civil war or collapse.[13] This development is of vital significance for a range of peacekeeping activities, as outlined in greater detail below.

Increased Size. The first obvious new quality is the scale of many UN missions. The 'big three' UN operations — the United Nations Transitional Authority in Cambodia (UNTAC), the United Nations Protection Force in the former Yugoslavia (UNPROFOR), and the second United Nations Operation in Somalia (UNOSOM II) — all deployed close to or more than 20,000 personnel at some point during the mission. Before these missions, only the United Nations Operation in the Congo approached this size. In addition, several other recently established UN operations involve more than 6,000 personnel, including the UN Confidence Restoration Operation (Croatia) (UNCRO), the United Nations Mission in Haiti (UNMIH), and the United Nations Mission for Rwanda (UNAMIR). The increased size of these missions has implications for command and control, financial arrangements, and availability of contributions.

Operation in Hostile Environments. In addition, many UN missions are now being conducted in more dangerous or 'less permissive' environments. In many cases, UN contingents are operating in a theatre where they do not have the consent of the local parties. Peacekeeping personnel are encountering obstruction, armed attack, threats, and even kidnapping as they attempt to carry out their mission. They are also being deployed into areas of virtual anarchy and civil disorder. Increasingly, mission tasks must be carried out in areas with active paramilitary groups or armed factions with limited discipline and often no political control. As a result, peacekeeping missions have suffered increased fatalities and injuries to UN personnel.

Attempting to Create a Peace. The function of UN peacekeeping personnel has also undergone a fundamental shift with respect to the conditions surrounding their deployment. Rather than being deployed to reinforce or maintain an existing political arrangement, UN contingents are now operating in environments where no such agreement exists, with the aim of dissuading the combatants from fighting.[14] The new trend is for the UN to use military force to compel the parties to cease fighting or to change their political and military conduct, a very different proposition from what guided traditional peacekeeping missions.

Proliferation of Mission Tasks. What is often lost in the public attention devoted to the military component of the big three is the change in the scope of the mission of most UN operations. Contemporary UN missions are now undertaking a much wider variety of tasks than were undertaken in Cold War peacekeeping operations. As Boutros Boutros-Ghali has pointed out, it is now "almost always the case that operations undertaken by the United Nations, must include civilian police, electoral personnel, human rights experts, information specialists, and a significant number of political advisory staff."[15] These tasks include the following:

- electoral support or management (the UN was heavily engaged in the election process in Cambodia);
- reform of judiciary and law enforcement authority (the UN was involved in judicial reform in El Salvador);
- refugee resettlement;
- securing a safe environment for the delivery of humanitarian relief supplies (this was an important component of the mission in UNPROFOR and UNOSOM I and II);
- disarmament of factions and weapons storage (this was conducted in the former Yugoslavia and in Somalia);
- mine clearing and education (with an estimated 100 million land mines deployed and two million more buried each year, mines pose an enormous obstacle to UN efforts in many countries;[16]
- protection of safe areas (this has been done to protect certain populations in the former Yugoslavia and represents a significant change in the territorial mission of peacekeeping personnel).

UN missions are therefore increasingly multi-component (or, as the UN says, multidimensional or multifunctional), with more and more responsibilities, demanding more and more co-operation with relief agencies and other non-governmental organizations.[17] Along with this have come the increased co-ordination difficulties that arise from such varied tasks and co-operation with other organizations.

The Importance of Force. The military aspect of peacekeeping has been enhanced. The threat to use force has been given a higher profile and role in the conduct of PKOs. Accordingly, UN peacekeeping contingents are now more heavily armed. Instead of being deployed with light personal weapons for use in self-defence, peacekeeping personnel are now equipped with most of their high-intensity warfare equipment, including heavy support weapons and armoured fighting vehicles. UN peacekeepers are also often buttressed by air and naval support. Despite this heavier armament, however, if peacekeeping forces are deployed in insufficient numbers, they will not be able to perform their roles through a mere presence. In the conduct of PKOs, firepower cannot substitute for numbers. Similarly, if peacekeeping forces are deployed with heavier armament but lack the mandate to use it, this armament becomes meaningless and in fact becomes a liability as a symbol of powerlessness.

Peacebuilding and National Reconstruction. Many mission tasks have an additional long-term objective: reconstruction of a viable, operational, and peaceful country, including the construction of working state structures, the creation of a democratic political process, and the entrenchment of law and civil society. In the case of countries that have suffered authoritarian or totalitarian regimes, this means the reform or redesign of the state apparatus and the political process; in the case of countries that have experienced a total collapse into anarchy, this entails the establishment of order, institutions, and government.

This extraordinarily ambitious process is based on the belief that establishing ceasefires or even peace is not enough; the underlying conditions for peace must be created if intervention is to be meaningful over the long term. As Boutros Boutros-Ghali has put it, "UN operations now may involve nothing less than the reconstruction of an entire society and state. This requires a *comprehensive* approach, over an extended period. Security is increasingly understood to involve social, economic, political, and cultural aspects far beyond its traditional military dimension."[18] Second generation peacekeeping is therefore closely linked to development issues and to regional confidence-building efforts.[19] This has had tremendous implications for the makeup of peacekeeping missions, which must have a wider variety of expertise available and must co-ordinate more frequently and more closely with non-governmental organizations in what the Canadian International Peacekeeping Training Centre calls the "new peacekeeping partnership". This demands increasing co-ordination between military, police, and civilian personnel.

PEACEKEEPING'S TIME OF TROUBLES: GENERAL IMPLICATIONS

The UN and the Credibility Dilemma

Images of Failure and Doubts About the Future. What has become increasingly evident from observations of UN operations — in particular the big three — is that the problems encountered by these missions are threatening the credibility of the UN as a conflict management instrument. While it would be premature to discard the concept of peacekeeping after the Cold War, it is nevertheless true that peace enforcement operations have been a spectacular failure in some instances. The UN is caught in an unfortunate credibility dilemma. The dilemma lies in the need to demonstrate its ability to respond constructively to ethnic conflict, civil strife and humanitarian crises — and so act as an agent of international conflict management after the Cold War — and the danger of managing such efforts poorly and demonstrating its inability to handle such problems. On one hand, the credibility of the UN depends on the ability to address the problems of the post-Cold War world. Should it prove unable or unwilling to respond to these problems, its relevance for the post-Cold War world will be questioned. This includes peacekeeping operations as well as collective security operations. As Boutros Boutros-Ghali wrote in *Agenda for Peace*, "While [military action] should only be taken when all peaceful means have failed, the option of taking it is essential to the credibility of the United Nations as a guarantor of international security."[20] On the other hand, the credibility of the United Nations is at risk when its operations meet setbacks and problems. The UN's credibility will be damaged if its interventions are unsuccessful. Not to engage in certain places or to permit some tragedies to continue unabated will lead to accusations of failure; to engage everywhere with mixed or unfortunate results exposes the limitations of the organization and also exposes it to accusations of failure.

The Lack of Political Will and the Credibility of the UN. Not to be overlooked is the fact that member states can make statements at the UN or provide minimal resources to UN efforts to create the illusion of commitment when in fact their level of commitment is not very high. For Rwanda, a request for 5,500 troops was issued by Boutros-Ghali on May 16, and no state — including those that were members of the standby force arrangement — replied. It was not until the end of July that 550 troops were despatched to Rwanda; by then, 500,000 people had been killed. The credibility of the UN is tied to this question of member state commitment, for if member countries do not demonstrate political will and commitment to the UN, the UN cannot succeed; and if it does not succeed, member states will be less disposed to work within or contribute to the UN.

Lack of a Suitable Mandate or Doctrine

New Missions, Old Doctrines. First, peace enforcement operations, which are by their nature extremely ambitious, are being mounted without a clear operational mandate or doctrinal framework.[21] The result is that, unlike traditional peacekeeping operations, where participants became familiar over time with the informal 'rules' governing such operations, national contingents are now deployed with unsuitable mandates and without a clear conception of the relationship between mission aims and operational conduct. For example, in the early stages of UNPROFOR, UN contingents had a mandate to use force only in self-defence, which made it impossible to respond to the realities of attacks on locals, refugees, and towns. This made UNPROFOR impotent and vulnerable to accusations of immorality.

Moreover, UN operations have shown a recent trend toward shifting and changing mandates and aims — often referred to as 'mission creep' — which may prove inconsistent with the original mission parameters under which some member states' contributions were offered. The UN and its member states will have to pass through a learning process similar to the one that developed the rules governing traditional peacekeeping operations. The old Chapter Six-and-a-half realm has been transcended, and as yet member states have been reluctant — except in Somalia — to invoke Chapter VII. A 'Chapter Six-and-three-quarters' concept must emerge to guide UN operations, and this may be possible only through long experience requiring time — a luxury the UN almost certainly does not have in light of the credibility dilemma it faces.

No Doctrine, No Unity. One of the consequences of the lack of a solid doctrinal foundation is the development of a divide over the nature and conduct of UN operations. As member state contingents are deployed without a clear conception of the nature of the mission, they naturally differ over aims and operational conduct. These differences occur largely because some contingents adhere to traditional peacekeeping practices while others seek to move beyond them, or because mission tasks change and contingents deployed under one mandate are reluctant to engage in newly assigned tasks. In other cases, mission mandates are so vague that they lead to disputes over their operational execution. This occurred in Somalia, where the 32-nation force was often divided about the nature of operations, especially with respect to the capture of Mohammed Farrah Aideed and the coercive disarmament of Somalia's warring factions. The effort to co-ordinate policy in Bosnia, especially with respect to air strikes, has led to numerous public and private disagreements. Differing conceptions can result in operations plagued by poor co-ordination and slow response times, with some contingents prepared to do some tasks while others are not. The possibility of increasing unco-ordination and perhaps friction between the contingents of peacekeeping operations, at both the political and the operational level, does not bode well for the success of future efforts.

Increased Great Power Involvement

A Great Power Game? UN peacekeeping operations have witnessed increased great power involvement. During the Cold War, the great powers seldom became involved in peacekeeping operations, not only because they were seldom seen as neutral in regional conflicts in the context of the Cold War, but also because it was often in the interests of the great powers to remain uninvolved. Great powers have recently become engaged in peacekeeping and peace enforcement because these regional conflicts are the central security concerns at present, and having been elevated to the status of threats to international peace and stability, they attract the interest of the great powers, which are sensitive to issues of order after the Cold War. In addition, because dealing with many of these conflicts has required military resources only the great powers can deploy, great power involvement has been seen increasingly as indispensable to the operational component of UN missions and to their political credibility.

Implications for Traditional Donors. The implications of this latter development for the traditional peacekeeping players — small states and middle powers — are worrisome. For these states, the concern lies in the loss of a foreign policy niche, role, or independent course in the conduct of their foreign affairs. Small states are facing the possibility that they may be less involved and perhaps submerged politically in missions that were once an important reflection of their foreign policy independence. While it would be premature to suggest that peacekeeping has become a great power game, the evolving situation bodes ill for states that were attracted to the enterprise because the great powers were not involved. It may also bode ill for the enterprise of peacekeeping itself; many traditional donors may be less disposed to involve themselves in operations alongside the great powers, especially after Somalia and Bosnia. Finally, to the extent that peace enforcement operations require larger, heavier forces and logistics capabilities, small states may either feel unable to make a meaningful contribution or will begin to expect the great powers to attend to international crises on their own.

UN Overstretch and Entrapment

Doing Too Much in Too Many Places: Peacekeeping Fatigue. There is concern that the UN has become overstretched or bogged down in too many intractable, open-ended missions. Peacekeeping is in more use than ever before. In 1987 the UN ran five operations with some 10,000 soldiers, at a cost of $233 million U.S. In mid-1993, there were 13 active peacekeeping operations, deploying some 70,000 personnel, at a cost of some $4 billion U.S. annually. In the summer of 1995, the UN was operating 16 peacekeeping missions involving more than 58,000 personnel.[22] Although these numbers fell to 29,140 by February 1996, over-engagement continues to be a problem, particularly for an organization already struggling for personnel, logistics, and funding.[23]

The funding element (a perpetual problem at the UN) has once again reached crisis proportions. In August 1995, the UN regular operations budget ran out of money, and the organization was forced to borrow some $98 million U.S. from the peacekeeping budget to meet regular budget outlays. Member states are now $2.7 billion U.S. in arrears to the UN regular and peacekeeping budgets.[24] The UN has also had trouble maintaining its peacekeeping payroll and owes $1.4 billion U.S. to peacekeeping contributors.[25] (To keep such expenditures in context, the entire UN budget for security-related functions is equivalent to the annual budget of the New York City police and fire departments combined.)

Exacerbating this problem is the question of the commitment of member states. The changing nature and greater cost of peacekeeping operations — in both financial terms and with respect to casualties — is giving countries second thoughts about contributing to existing and future efforts. As Boutros Boutros-Ghali has warned, "Our renaissance remains in question; demands made upon the United Nations are not being matched by the resources to do the job."[26] The failure to articulate clear exit strategies — that is, the conditions for terminating a UN operation — leaves open the possibility of long involvement in potentially hostile circumstances, a possibility few member countries have been willing to entertain. Ultimately, these developments have tarnished both peacemaking and peacekeeping to the point that member countries — even those with a long peacekeeping tradition — are reviewing their peacekeeping policies. Not only is the UN in danger of losing governmental support, it is also in danger of losing support from the publics of contributing states, who will not long tolerate governments expending resources and lives on conflicts far away. This 'peacekeeping fatigue' may have dire consequences for future UN efforts.

A Backlash Against Peace Operations? Several elements may combine to create a reaction, or backlash, against further attempts by the UN to mount peace enforcement missions:

- perceptions of UN failure in the big three operations (Cambodia, Somalia, and Yugoslavia);
- dissatisfaction with the UN's ability to respond in a timely and effective manner to international contingencies;
- a turn to unilateral or coalition conflict management efforts, largely outside the UN (such as the Contact Group); and
- the establishment of stricter criteria at the national level regarding involvement in UN operations.

In the face of these political and economic problems, member states and the leadership of the UN itself may be increasingly unwilling to mount new operations, especially large and costly operations of the peace enforcement variety. Unfortunately, the poor experience with many recent UN peace enforcement operations and the current fiscal climate may also constrain the ability of the UN to mount more modest missions of the traditional variety. There is a danger that traditional peacekeeping will be thrown out with the peace enforcement bathwater. Furthermore, sentiments such as these may result in the UN withdrawing from certain missions prematurely. Some have argued that the UN withdrew too rapidly from Cambodia and Angola.[27] The future resilience of the UN is therefore in question; will the UN be able to stay in situations that become complex, or will it withdraw when a situation becomes difficult, or when a more forceful action might succeed?

Preserving the Tested Mechanism. Will traditional peacekeeping operations come to be tarred with the peace enforcement brush? While the UN has encountered many difficulties, particularly in two of its largest (and most publicized) operations in Somalia and Yugoslavia, many other UN missions have been proceeding with more success. The problems encountered in the big three UN operations should not be taken as indicative of the applicability of traditional peacekeeping in the future. Traditional peacekeeping should not be discarded as irrelevant after the Cold

War; its provisions are likely to remain valuable irrespective of the future of peace enforcement operations.[28] Traditional peacekeeping may be suited to many contingencies in the future. In addition, traditional peacekeeping missions are conducted at a level of involvement at which member countries are willing to supply their own personnel. In the absence of consensus on the violability of sovereignty, traditional peacekeeping principles maintain a set of standards for involvement that limit UN over-extension and limit the potential for damaging setbacks.

The UN as a Participant in Hostilities. In many conflicts, the United Nations has become a party in the dispute among hostile warring factions. Indeed, the UN has become a participant in these disputes, no longer regarded as a neutral, impartial third party but seen as another actor in a conflict to be accounted for in political, strategic and tactical calculations. The UN has been dragged further and further into such conflicts as it has sought to establish its aims with successive escalations of the size and scope of its involvement. Of course, each escalation (and deployment of resources) has served only to increase the commitment of the UN to achieving its aims and made it more difficult for the UN to contract operations, withdraw or admit failure. This has subjected UN forces to attack and to obstruction of their mission aims. When this occurs, UN contingents react predictably, treating the locals as 'the enemy' and further eroding the relationship between UN personnel and the local population.

The UN may also find itself caught up in the politics of separatist movements. Although this has occurred in the past, the UN is involving itself in more intrastate conflicts, many of which by their nature have a separatist element. The quandary for the UN is that failure to intervene in separatist-held areas — or a decision to leave them — may be seen as passing judgement on the legitimacy of a separatist cause.

UN Marginalization

The Loss of Political and Operational Control and the Role of the United States. The United Nations is in danger of losing operational control over the missions it establishes or sanctions. Here, the relationship with the United States will be critical. One of the greatest problems confronting the UN is the management of its relations with its most powerful member, a member that is increasingly sceptical of the UN's abilities and the value of working with it.[29] Despite recent developments with respect to the Clinton administration's peacekeeping policy and the attitudes of the Republican-dominated Congress — which suggest a more restrictive approach to UN peace operations and a more unilateral approach to international contingencies — there must be a concern that the United States is exercising greater influence, some might even say dominance, over UN peace operations.[30] This can occur in one of three ways: the United States can be involved in the operation itself and exert great influence on the nature of the mission, as it did in Somalia; the United States can engage in activities or make decisions with a bearing on the conduct of missions of which it is not a part, as it has with respect to the peace process and the airstrike option in Bosnia; or the United States can obtain UN sanction for a U.S.-dominated mission, as in Haiti. Nor is the United States the only country doing this; Russia deployed forces in Abkhazia under Security Council authority but not under its supervision.

The Influence of the United States. U.S. involvement is seen increasingly as a condition for the success of many UN operations. However, even as the success of such operations may depend more on U.S. involvement, the willingness of the United States to become involved will depend on the extent to which U.S. conditions (in the form of greater control over operations and mission mandates) are met. The operation in Somalia turned this corner with the activation of Operation Restore Hope and the Unified Task Force (UNITAF) under U.S. command. The operation in Somalia became heavily Americanized, reigniting concerns that had smouldered since the Gulf War about the extent to which the UN had become a provider of political or moral sanction for U.S. policy. Attending this danger is another concern; as the UN becomes more dependent on the United States, the UN will become increasingly subject to shifts in U.S. policy. This has already caused problems in Somalia and Bosnia. Furthermore, greater reliance on the United States also creates a problem of sustaining UN operations should the United States withdraw. If the United States becomes the UN's fire brigade — rushing to and fro stabilizing problematic UN operations — maintaining order after it has gone will be difficult for less well equipped (and possibly less numerous) peacekeepers.

Contracting Out. Another concern is the recent trend toward reliance on regional organizations to conduct UN peace enforcement operations. The most prominent example is NATO action in Bosnia. While 'contracting out' may offer a means of relieving some of the financial and personnel pressures on the UN, it implies that these regional organizations, relying on their own command and control mechanisms, will have virtually complete operational control over peacekeeping or peace enforcement missions, with little or no input from the UN at anything but a high political level. Whether this dissociation of UN political authority and operational control can be managed remains to be seen. Furthermore, regional organizations may themselves be plagued with disputes over political direction and operational execution. Traditional small-state or middle-power peacekeepers that belong to such organizations may find themselves dragged into policy positions they find undesirable by pressures for alliance unity. For traditional peacekeepers that are not members of NATO or a regional organization involved in peacekeeping or peace enforcement, the prospects for input or influence are rather grim.

Wars of Conscience and the CNN Factor

Intervention on Humanitarian Grounds: A New Norm? Might there be a growing intolerance of gross human rights abuses, an intolerance that is leading to the erosion of state sovereignty as a barrier to righteous interventions in such cases?[31] Cold War examples of humanitarian intervention — India in East Pakistan (1971), Vietnam in Cambodia (1978), and Tanzania in Uganda (1979) — were stained by the evident political interests of the intervening parties. However, a recent trend toward humanitarian intervention seems to exist; witness the operations in Northern Iraq, Haiti, Liberia, Tadjikistan, Cambodia, the former Yugoslavia, Somalia, and Rwanda. The gross human rights violations (and general human suffering) evident in these cases prompted international intervention on the grounds that they posed a threat to international peace and security. Explanations ranged from the moralistic to the geopolitical. Wrongs had to be stopped or conflicts contained to prevent spillover.

This represented a shift of some significance, for it appeared as if the principles of sovereignty and non-intervention were being eroded, that human rights were acquiring some objective value that states had a duty to uphold, and that states were beginning to distinguish between the rights of the state and the rights of the people residing within it. There has been increased recognition of the human rights abuses perpetrated in El Salvador, Guatemala, Indonesia, China, and many other states, and greater attention paid to the International Bill of Human Rights (which includes the Universal Declaration and separate covenants on political rights, economic rights, and social rights). Although the Universal Declaration is not a vehicle for outright intervention, it serves as a mechanism for scrutiny, as any signatory is bound by the treaty and cannot therefore declare this area a matter of domestic jurisdiction. There may also be a shift in public attitudes toward the view that conflict and human rights should prevail over borders and legal documents, a shift brought about by graphic media reports of these humanitarian disasters.

Finally, there is concern that the UN convention of attempting nonforcible sanctions before attempting more forceful action has compromised past opportunities to intervene early to contain conflicts (e.g., Yugoslavia and Haiti) and prevent hostilities from spiralling out of control.[32]

A Blueprint for Intervention? A body of thought has developed that intends to lay the foundation for norms of international intervention in cases of civil strife or human rights abuses. In this view, sovereignty should convey not only rights but duties, which include human rights and protection from suffering. In cases of human rights abuses, the sovereignty of the rights of peoples overrides the sovereignty of the state. As Swedish Prime Minister Ingvar Carlsson has argued, "To confine the concept of security exclusively to the protection of states is to ignore the interests of people in whose name sovereignty is exercised."[33]

In this view, the international community has a duty to respond to human suffering and human rights abuses. The principle of non-intervention can be used to prevent legitimate action out of concern for human rights and human suffering, and therefore the balance between the protection of sovereignty and the protection of human rights should be tipped in favour of human rights. Intervention would be justified under the following conditions: when states are unwilling or unable to protect their populations; when state authorities can be held responsible for abuses and human suffering on a large scale; when victims appeal for international assistance; and when intervention can succeed in addressing the problem.

There are of course serious obstacles in the way of such an international norm on intervention. Foremost among these is the grim experience of many humanitarian intervention efforts, especially in Somalia and Rwanda. These experiences may have served to turn governments and publics against intervention in light of past failures and the costs — both human and financial — associated with them. Other obstacles include uncertainty about the source of financial resources for intervention; the jealousy with which states guard their sovereignty (five countries from the developing world voted against resolution 688 on the grounds that it weakened sovereignty and violated the Charter); concern about getting involved in quagmires; and questions about who sets the standards, who verifies them, and ultimately who intervenes.

Humanitarian Intervention and 'Spasm' Responses. And yet, political commitment to human rights violations has not been universal or particularly strong. In the past, gross violations of human rights have failed to bring on a large public or governmental response (for example in Burundi and Rwanda, Cambodia, and Guatemala). In more contemporary cases, egregious examples such as Rwanda failed to provoke a timely response, while others — in Syria, Bangladesh, Indonesia and Uganda, among others — have failed to gain much attention at all. It would seem that the intolerance to human rights abuses — and to human suffering of any kind — is highly selective. Why is this? As pointed out in Chapter 1, there has always been a tension between the principle of state sovereignty and freedom from interference, and this is especially the case with respect to human rights. While the UN Charter calls for respect of human rights (article 1), it goes on to state (in article 2) that "All members shall refrain in their international relations from the threat or use of force against the territorial integrity or the political independence of any state" and that "Nothing contained in the present Charter shall authorize the UN to intervene in matters which are essentially within the domestic jurisdiction of any state." For the most part the state has been the victor in the tension between sovereignty and human rights. Of course, traditional power politics and national interests play a role in international responses. As a result, the pattern of intervention was subject to political and ideological imperatives. A recent phenomenon has also emerged that stands as a partial explanation of the 'spasm' response of the international community to cases of humanitarian need and gross human rights violations.

The CNN Factor. The impact of television, and the political power of images, has been very clear in the international response to the crises in the former Yugoslavia and Somalia. Media images of starving people, squalid conditions, dead civilians, and interference by warring parties, local officials, or bandit elements have caused outrage and an outpouring of humanitarian concern and aid. They have also prompted or facilitated the commitment of national governments to UN efforts to bring an end to these conflicts and to human suffering. However, this 'CNN factor' is double-edged; it can encourage and promote international responses to cases of human suffering, but it can also have two opposite effects. First, the CNN factor is by its nature reactive and selective. It can do nothing to prevent such incidents, and reaction to images often takes place at the height rather than the beginning of a crisis, when it is less manageable or, in some cases, too late to address. Furthermore, the international response it provokes is extended only to the case that appeared in the media; other cases, possibly just as deserving, are not addressed or responded to. In addition, media attention is fleeting. This creates a problem of sustainability, a problem recognized by humanitarian aid efforts, which must be concerned with "how to provide humanitarian sustenance after the initial outpouring of international concern has subsided and humanitarian interests are left to vie with other causes for the international spotlight."[34] Second, the same, largely emotional, reaction that prompted action can provoke resentment and opposition to national involvement as well. This occurred in Somalia, when images of the bodies of dead U.S. personnel being mistreated provoked an outcry and calls for U.S. withdrawal. The CNN factor can therefore have the following impact:

- It can lead to short-term, 'spasm' responses rather than long-term solutions to long-term problems.
- It can focus international attention only on places or events where the media are present.
- It can distort perceptions of the problem and fails to convey detail or context.
- It can lead to dramatic swings in public opinion and government responses, with negative consequences for measured, long-term policies.
- It can lead to perceptions of UN incompetence by focusing on dramatic failures and failing to convey less spectacular but important successes.
- It can be manipulated or used as a propaganda instrument by the parties to a conflict.

Following on the discussion in Chapter 2 of the importance of information and perception in future conflicts and intervention efforts, it is imperative that UN peace operations and contributing governments have a media strategy when embarking on such missions.

Future Challenges to PKOs and Operational Requirements

What will be required to enable UN peace operations to confront the emerging threat created by the changing nature of conflict identified in Chapter 2? New situations create new demands on personnel and capabilities. If future UN peace operations are to be effective, the demands placed on them must be anticipated and taken into account. The examination conducted for this study suggests that future missions must acquire, or improve, their capabilities in the following areas:

- improved co-ordination and co-operation between civilian and military organizations and personnel, with a view to establishing clear and effective lines of communication and consultation;
- improved understanding/intelligence of the political, ethnic, and religious dimensions of a conflict and an improved capacity for intelligence gathering at all levels;
- improved capacity to engage in information warfare and combat propaganda campaigns;
- the development of effective public information campaigns in contributor countries on the reasons for and conduct of the mission;
- improved supplementary training on maintenance of order functions, such as detainment, crowd control, and enforcement of law and order;
- improved technical capacity to manage riots and unruly individuals short of lethal force;
- enhanced engineering capability for infrastructure and works projects;
- implementation of deployment and patrol procedures to minimize vulnerability of personnel to hostage taking or terrorist acts;
- rules of engagement (ROEs) adjusted to account for riots, looters, banditry, thievery, snipers and other incidents outside political control. ROEs must be simple and direct;
- ROEs for forcible disarmament and weapons cantonment;
- awareness of and preparation for possible encounters with chemical and biological weapons; and
- creation of a national pool of qualified civilian, police, and military personnel and capabilities available for specialized tasks.

CHAPTER SUMMARY

1. The post-Cold War UN agenda is very broad, but it is the security role of the institution that will be the most prominent in estimations of the organization's future.
2. UN peacekeeping missions have changed dramatically, with many of the conventions of traditional peacekeeping swept aside. Peace enforcement efforts have a number of new qualities that distinguish them from traditional peacekeeping efforts:

- They are often larger efforts, with UNOSOM II, UNTAC, and UNPROFOR numbering more than 20,000 at some point.
- They are operating in 'less permissive' environments, often without the consent of all the parties, in which the local population and UN personnel may come to regard each other through suspicious or hostile eyes or even as 'the enemy'.
- They are attempting to create conditions for peace, rather than keep a peace already in place.
- They are more multi-component, performing a much wider variety of mission tasks, encompassing military, police, development, aid, and civilian administrative functions.
- The use of force has become an increasingly important component of UN missions.
- They are engaging in long-term national reconstruction or peacebuilding tasks, which tend to be more ambitious in scope than efforts conducted by peacekeeping missions.

3. This has resulted in a time of troubles for peacekeeping. These troubles include:

- a serious credibility problem;
- a lack of suitable mandates or doctrines for the conduct of peace enforcement operations;
- increased great power involvement;
- a UN that is overstretched and bogged down in too many missions;
- a marginalized UN, in danger of losing operational command and control over UN missions; and
- the appropriateness and modalities of humanitarian intervention and the power of the CNN factor.

4. The effectiveness of future UN efforts will increasingly depend on the following requirements:

- improved co-ordination and co-operation between civilian and military organizations and personnel, with a view to establishing clear and effective lines of communication and consultation;
- improved understanding/intelligence of the political, ethnic, and religious dimensions of a conflict;
- improved capacity for intelligence gathering at all levels;
- improved capacity to engage in information warfare and combat propaganda campaigns;

- the development of effective public information campaigns in contributor countries on the reasons for and conduct of the mission;
- improved supplementary training on maintenance of order functions such as detainment, crowd control, and enforcement of law and order;
- improved technical capacity to manage riots and unruly individuals short of lethal force;
- enhanced engineering capability for infrastructure and works projects;
- implementation of deployment and patrol procedures to minimize vulnerability of personnel to hostage taking or terrorist acts;
- ROEs adjusted to account for riots, looters, banditry, thievery, snipers and other incidents outside political control; ROEs must be simple and direct;
- ROEs for forcible disarmament and weapons cantonment;
- awareness of and preparation for possible encounters with chemical and biological weapons; and
- creation of a national pool of qualified civilian, police, and military personnel and capabilities available for specialized tasks.

CHAPTER FOUR

The United Nations and Somalia: Lessons and Implications

THE NATURE OF THE CONFLICT IN SOMALIA

The Legacies of the Past: Somalia's History and Social Structure

Early History. The Somali peoples have an ancient history; archaeological evidence suggests that they had occupied the Horn of Africa by 100 AD.[1] They were primarily nomadic herders and moved into surrounding areas in a great wave of migration beginning in the tenth century in search of pastureland and arable areas. The harsh environment brought them into conflict with one another over resources (primarily water and land), and migration brought them into conflict with other peoples (primarily the Oromo and Galla peoples). The Somali peoples have also been subject to various rulers, including Oman, Zanzibar, the sharifs of Mukha, and the Ottoman Empire. In the middle of the nineteenth century Somalia was controlled by the British, French, and Italian empires, as well as by Ethiopia, although the British and Italians would dominate the administration of Somalia through British Somaliland in the north and Italian Somaliland in the south. Imperial rule was characterized by resistance; the Dervish struggle against foreign domination lasted from 1900 to 1920. As a result, the history of the Somali peoples is largely martial, one of warfare and resistance to foreign domination, with warrior traditions held in high regard. Foreign rule, and the partition of the country into British and Italian possessions, was to last until 1960, although the last 10 years were under UN trusteeship, with Italy as the administering authority.

The Clans. Although significant communities of Somali-speaking peoples live outside the borders of Somalia, in Ethiopia, Djibouti and Kenya,

Somalia is characterized by a high degree of domestic homogeneity. The population is almost entirely Somali in origin and shares common language, religious (Islam), and cultural traditions. The Somali peoples constitute one of the largest ethnic groups in Africa. Despite this ethnic and religious unity, the predominant characteristic of Somali social structure is the division and patterns of relations between clans, family aggregations rooted in traditional territories and in generational lineages that can be traced for hundreds of years. The clan structure of the modern Somali has many levels of division, beginning with the Samaal and the Sab. The former include the majority of Somalis and are divided into four major clans, the Dir, Isaaq, Hawiye, and Darod, which share predominantly pastoral/ nomadic traditions. The Sab, composed of the Dighil and Rahanwyn clans, share predominantly agricultural/cultivation traditions.[2] These clans are further divided into sub-clans, which have their own patterns of enmity and amity, with conflict between sub-clans of the same clan not unusual. Further, loyalty within clans and sub-clans is localized, with loyalty to individuals dissipating the further they live from immediate family.[3] Clan and sub-clan disputes centre around control of territory, wells, and pastureland. Traditionally, authority in Somali society rests not only with the heads of the clans and sub-clans, but with clan elders, who play important roles in the areas of dispute management and justice, in which the concept of compensation for grievances is central.

Clan Conflict and the State. The independent Somali Republic was formed on 1 July 1960 by the merger of the former British Somaliland (which gained its independence on 26 June 1960) and Italian Somaliland. Clan rivalry and conflict (as well as alliances and co-operation) have had a profound impact on the domestic politics of the Somali state. The colonial administrations and the parliamentary state system installed after independence had three effects: one was to marginalize the authority of the clan elders, especially with respect to conflict management; a second was the atomization of the party system and the increasing convergence between party divisions and clan divisions; and a third was the creation of another arena of conflict between clans and sub-clans as they competed for position and influence in state structures in an effort to gain control of the resources of the state. This became a core issue, for the Somali state has been heavily dependent on foreign disbursements and aid, and control of the dissemination and use of this aid came to be an important foundation of power.

Somali Nationalism under Dictatorial Rule. In October 1969, a military coup led by Major-General Mohammed Siad Barre overthrew Somalia's first president, Abdirashiid Ali Schermaarke. Barre banned political opposition, implemented a centrally managed political and economic system based on socialist models, and strengthened the armed forces by importing a vast stock of weapons. Official ideology was linked closely to the development of a socialist nationalism in an effort to establish loyalty to the Barre regime. This effort included literacy and propaganda campaigns, suppression of expressions of clan and Islamic loyalties, efforts to replace the role of elders and clan leaders with state personnel, and expansionist policies aimed at uniting with Somalis outside Somalia's borders. In 1977, the Barre regime attacked Ethiopia, in an effort to seize the disputed Ogaden region. The war ended, a year later, with Somalia's defeat. The war had two consequences: it was the catalyst for growing opposition to Barre's rule, and it served to draw yet more armaments into the country. In an effort to retain power, Barre began to rely heavily on the army and the favour of three sub-clans within the Darod, to which Barre and the majority of his relatives belonged. Other clans were subjected to political and economic marginalization. Barre also attempted to suppress other clans through violence, including the mass murder of other clans' elites.[4] This led to the mobilization of most clans against the Barre government. By the mid-1980s, organized opposition to the Barre government had emerged, which spread and intensified as the government engaged in increasingly violent reprisals.

The Collapse

The Provisional Government and the Collapse of the State. Siad Barre was overthrown by force on 27 January 1991 by a combination of opposition movements and their militias, organized along clan lines (see Table 4.1). The United Somali Congress (USC), based on the Hawiye clan, and the Somali National Movement (SNM), based on the Isaaq clan, announced the formation of a provisional government on 2 February 1991, with Ali Mahdi Mohammed of the Hawiye as president and Umar Arteh Ghalib of the Isaaq as prime minister. However, Mahdi became president of a state that had virtually ceased to exist in the final years of Siad Barre's rule.[5] The armed forces had fractured along clan lines, and the police, bureaucracy, schools, and medical system had virtually disappeared. Infrastructure had been heavily damaged in the fighting to overthrow Barre, and retreating Barre loyalists had slaughtered livestock and plundered crops in southern Somalia, contributing to a widening famine brought on by drought and the devastation of war. The disintegration of the state continued under the provisional government, which was unable to achieve any degree of unity among the clan factions. The opposition clans had only the defeat of Barre in common, and there was also resentment and suspicion toward the Hawiye clan for acquiring so much power in post-Barre Somalia. The Hawiye also failed to consult other clans in forming the government.[6] Clashes between rival clans broke out as each turned to force to achieve its aims of influence in the post-Barre government. This new round of fighting resulted in the complete disintegration of the few state services still functional, and much of the countryside and the capital, Mogadishu, became battlegrounds.

Table 4.1
Somalia's Warring Factions

	Clan	*Sub-Clan*	*Political Faction*
Samaal	Darod		
		Marehan (Morgan)	Somalia National Front (SNF)
		Ogaden (Jess)	Somalia Patriotic Movement (SPM)
		Majerteen	S. Salvation Democratic Front (SSDF)
		Dolbuhante	United Somalia Party (USP)
		Warsengeli	United Somalia Party (USP)
	Hawiye		United Somali Congress (USC)
		Abgal (Mahdi)	Manifesto Group
		Habar Gedir (Aideed)	Somalia National Alliance (SNA)
	Issaq		Somalia National Movement (SNM)
	Dir	Issa	United Somalia Front (USF)
		Godabursi	Somalia Democratic Front (SDA)
Sab	Dighil		Somalia Democratic Movement (SDM)
	Rahenwein		Somalia Democratic Movement (SDM)

Intensification of Clan Conflict. For the next 16 months, factional fighting continued across Somalia and in Mogadishu. The pattern of conflict and co-operation across clan and sub-clan shifted regularly. The principal clan and sub-clan players and their associated political movements are listed in Table 4.1.[7] Not shown is the fact that sub-clans were themselves composed of sub-clans and that there was a complex relationship between these familial sub-clan groupings. There is some dispute in the literature as to the link between the clans/sub-clans and the political movements.

The two key figures in the battle for the control of the area around Mogadishu were Mohammed Farrah Aidid, who split from the United Somali Congress and formed the Somali National Alliance, and his main rival, President Ali Mahdi Mohammed, who formed the Manifesto Group of the USC. Also involved in the Mogadishu area were Mohammed Siad Hersi (General Morgan), son-in-law of Siad Barre and head of the Somali National Front (SNF), based around the Marehan clan, and Colonel Ahmed Omar Jess, head of the Somali Patriotic Movement (SPM), based around the Ogaden Clan. In the north, the Somali National Movement declared the independence of the former British Somaliland, which has yet to receive recognition within Somalia or from outside.[8] In addition to the violence between clans and sub-clans, conflict broke out between familial groups within sub-clans. Banditry (and local warlords) thrived in the absence of a central government and easy access to weapons.

The Humanitarian Disaster. The humanitarian disaster in Somalia was the result of two contributing factors: the warfare between the Barre government and the subsequent factional fighting between clans and sub-clans; and a period of severe drought. The result was starvation, a large refugee population, and a crippled recovery capacity. Above all, the tragedy that motivated international efforts in Somalia was starvation. UN officials warned in June 1992 that 1.5 million Somalis might starve to death, and that some 4.5 million Somalis, of a population of 7.7 million, were facing hunger.[9] Later reports suggested 100,000 Somalis had died from starvation and civil war, with 2 million more threatened with starvation.[10] At their peak, starvation rates ranged between 1,000 and 3,000 a day. By December 1992, it was estimated that the year's death toll from starvation was 400,000.[11] In addition, a large number of people, displaced by drought and war, had begun to move in search of relief. By mid-1992, close to one million people had become refugees, with the majority (some 700,000) fleeing to neighbouring countries.[12] Disease was also a major problem; by mid-1992 only 15 of Somalia's 70 hospitals were open, and these lacked even basic supplies.[13] Water treatment and distribution facilities ceased to function, and contaminated water contributed to outbreaks of diarrhoea, cholera, and typhoid epidemics.

Just as serious was the damage done to the ability to recover from the disaster. Cultivation recovery was damaged by the destruction of irrigation plants and facilities, seed stocks, storage facilities, and arable land. Livestock herds were depleted, through slaughter for food as a result of disease. This was particularly important in pastoral regions, where livestock was the basis of both wealth and diet. In addition, the recovery of herds takes several years, so serious depletion poses a long-term problem. Damage to infrastructure also posed an obstacle to recovery; economic activity was hampered by lack of communications, electricity, and formal banking facilities.

The Character of the Conflict in Somalia: A Factional Conflict

Somalia: Example of a Factional Intra-ethnic Conflict. Chapter 2 described some of the characteristics of the ethnic, religious and factional conflicts that beset the contemporary international system. Somalia exhibits many of the qualities of these conflicts:

- Somalia is an example of an intrastate, rather than an interstate conflict, occurring in a developing country.
- As a result, the central actors are sub-state groups.
- The sub-state actors in Somalia are clan-based factions, not ethnic groups or religious groups. Somalia can be described most accurately as an example of factional conflict.
- The origins of the conflict lie in efforts of various clans to alter domestic circumstances in the face of political and economic marginalization. The conflict is a struggle for political power.
- The civilian population was directly involved in the conflict and played a role in political and military strategies involving attacks on resources and expropriation of humanitarian aid.
- The conflict was conducted by largely irregular forces with no clear front, weak or irregular command and control, and widespread banditry.

SOMALIA AND PEACEMAKING AND PEACEBUILDING

The Initial UN Response

Relief Efforts and the Prelude to UNOSOM I. Despite the breakdown and eventual collapse of services and internal order between 1988 and late 1990, various UN aid agencies and non-governmental humanitarian relief organizations continued to function in Somalia. However, as the fighting to oust Barre intensified in January 1991, most embassy personnel, UN staff, and relief agencies were evacuated. Several NGOs remained behind and were the sole conduit for relief efforts in the early months of 1991.[14] This led to mounting public criticism of the UN in late 1991, including an unusual critique from the International Committee of the Red Cross.[15]

UN offices reopened in May and August, only to be closed and evacuated in November (and subsequently reopened in December) because of renewed fighting. Through 1991, relief agencies encountered progressively more serious obstacles in their efforts to deliver humanitarian relief supplies and services throughout the country. Among the most serious problems were these:

- threats to personal security (between October 1990 and January 1993, four members of the International Committee of the Red Cross were killed);
- theft of relief supplies (the UN Department of Humanitarian Affairs estimated that less than 20 per cent of aid was reaching the intended beneficiaries);
- logistics problems (closure of port facilities in Mogadishu and Kismayo, poor roads, interference by local clans and warlords); and
- extortion and blackmail (relief personnel were often compelled to pay — often with relief supplies — for protection and escorts).

By early 1992, the situation confronting UN and NGO agencies prompted a number of dire warnings to the UN and the world community about the extent of the disaster in Somalia.[16] The Organization of African Unity (OAU) and the League of Arab States (LAS) proved incapable of offering meaningful assistance to Somalia. Neighbouring OAU states, once threatened by Somalia, were unwilling to divert scarce resources to Somalia, and an LAS resolution calling for aid to Somalia amounted to nothing. In 1992, stung by the criticisms levelled against it in late 1991, the UN stepped up its efforts to address the Somalia situation. But it was hampered by 'crisis fatigue', brought on by the disasters in Sudan and Ethiopia and the conflict in the Persian Gulf. The UN sponsored preparatory talks on a national reconciliation conference among 14 Somali factions in early January. The UN Security Council imposed an arms embargo against Somalia on 23 January 1992,[17] although the impact of this embargo was questionable in light of the large stocks of weapons already in the country. The UN also successfully negotiated a ceasefire between the USC factions led by General Aideed and Mr. Ali Mahdi in Mogadishu. This ceasefire, signed on 3 March 1992, authorized the dispatch of an UN fact-finding team to Somalia and enabled the port to be opened to ships carrying humanitarian relief supplies for the first time in six months. The ceasefire did not affect conditions outside Mogadishu, nor did it solve the problem of banditry. Diplomatic efforts continued; in April, a meeting of heads of state in the Horn of Africa was convened in Addis Ababa to discuss regional co-operation in the Somalia crisis.

UNOSOM I: An Inadequate Response. On the basis of the UN fact-finding team's report and a proposal by the Secretary-General, the UN Operation in Somalia (UNOSOM) was established by the Security Council on 24 April 1992 (Resolution 751). The resolution was based on traditional peacekeeping precepts of impartiality, consent, and light armament; Somalia's warring factions called unanimously for a UN humanitarian assistance operation and recovery program. The resolution established a small UN observer force, consisting of 50 unarmed military personnel, which was to patrol a demarcation line between the combatants in Mogadishu. Later, an agreement in principle to the deployment of a security force numbering 500 personnel was negotiated.[18] However, the absence of a central government required the UN to seek the approval of the factions in Somalia to implement the mission. Opposition caused delays, particularly to the deployment of the 50 unarmed observers and the 500-member security force. The capital was the central concern of the new UN mission, although there was reference to other areas of the country and UNOSOM I was also committed to efforts to negotiate a general political settlement.

The observer force, under Pakistani General Imtiaz Shaheen, arrived in July 1992, although the security force component of UNOSOM I (a Pakistani contingent of 500 personnel) did not arrive until September. However, this force was unable to leave the harbour and airport areas of Mogadishu, as it did not have the consent of factional leaders in the

Mogadishu area to do so. Despite the official focus on the capital, the UN Special Representative of the Secretary General (SRSG) to Somalia, Mohammed Sahnoun, conducted extensive discussions with faction leaders throughout the country to build consensus on UNOSOM activities. There was growing frustration with the sluggish international response to the situation in Somalia, as well as the obstructionism of clan leaders and warlords, despite a pledge of co-operation from many factions at a conference convened in late May and early June in Bahir Dar, Ethiopia. In Resolution 767 of 27 July, the Security Council expressed its "concern" that the magnitude of human suffering in Somalia constituted "a threat to international peace and security" and authorized the use of all available means and arrangements to facilitate humanitarian efforts in Somalia. It also suggested that if co-operation from Somalia's factions was not forthcoming, other means of delivering humanitarian relief supplies would be considered.[19]

Expansion of the UNOSOM I Mandate. On 28 August 1992, under the terms of Security Council Resolution 775, the mandate of UNOSOM I was extended over other areas of the country. The mandate was also expanded to incorporate new tasks, which included humanitarian operations, the establishment of security for relief supplies, ceasefire monitoring, and disarmament. The mandated size of the force was expanded to 3,000 security personnel (including the unit of 500 already in the theatre), with a total authorized strength of 4,219 of all ranks.[20] However, this expansion was carried out without the approval or even consultation of Somalia's faction leaders.

This step marked an important departure point for the UN with respect to traditional Chapter VI peacekeeping. In Somalia, the UN effort was hamstrung by the continued requirement that UN operations be conducted with the approval of local authorities. Despite the earlier efforts of Sahnoun to establish a favourable environment in much of the countryside, in many areas this proved difficult, as local clan leaders and warlords frequently refused to allow UN security personnel to operate in their areas, or refused to honour prior agreements. For his part, Sahnoun had become increasingly upset with the level of support and commitment from New York and from UN agencies, and the expansion of UNOSOM I marked the end of his tenure as SRSG. The expansion of UNOSOM I had been announced without prior consultation with Sahnoun or the faction leaders in Somalia. Sahnoun had promised that such consultation would take place as part of his efforts to build the confidence of faction leaders. Sahnoun was compelled to resign on 27 October, and his replacement (by Ismat Kittani) and the provisions of Resolution 775 were seen by many in Somalia (especially General Aideed) as the prelude to a foreign invasion.

UNOSOM I also never reached its mandated strength in the field, because of the refusal of Somali factions to accept its deployment; in fact, by December 1992, UNOSOM I was composed of only 564 personnel, a force far too small to carry out the expanded mandate. The UN had also made little progress in achieving security for relief operations. Two incidents in November were particularly galling. When the Pakistani battalion moved to control Mogadishu's airport, they were instructed to leave and then fired upon by General Aideed's forces. Later in the month, despite an agreement with Ali Mahdi that relief vessels attempting to dock in Mogadishu would not be attacked, a World Food Program ship was shelled when it entered the port. By November 1992, then, the UN was looking very bad in Somalia, and credibility was becoming an important issue. Security for relief supplies had not improved, the famine was achieving widespread publicity, and clan leaders and warlords were flouting the UN's authority and efforts to achieve peace in the country.[21] More forceful measures and a larger presence were seen as the answer.

The Big Step: UNITAF and UNOSOM II

The Creation of UNITAF. In response to the situation, Boutros-Ghali acknowledged in late November that UNOSOM I was not adequate to the task, and on 30 November 1992 the Secretary-General called for "more forceful measures".[22] Media coverage of the crisis and the failings of the UN put pressure on the Bush administration to address the crisis. The United States indicated that it would be willing to organize, command, and lead a multilateral operation in Somalia if it was authorized to use force. In Resolution 794 of 3 December 1992, the Security Council authorized a U.S.-led Unified Task Force (UNITAF) for Somalia under Chapter VII of the UN Charter. The force was authorized to use "all necessary means to establish as soon as possible a secure environment for humanitarian relief operations in Somalia."[23]

UNITAF was conceived as a short-term operation, designed to secure a favourable environment for humanitarian relief efforts, then hand over responsibility to a follow-on UN operation. The three core objectives UNITAF sought to achieve were to control port facilities in Mogadishu and Kismayu; to open and secure supply routes and storage and logistics facilities across the country for the humanitarian relief effort; and to prepare the way for handing over responsibility for humanitarian relief operations to UNOSOM II.

Resolution 794 was unusual in several respects. The reference to Chapter VII authority was extraordinary under the circumstances (only Korea and the Gulf War stood as precedents). The escalation from a peacekeeping mission to the invocation of Chapter VII was entirely unique. The resolution also linked the three concepts of peace enforcement (under Chapter VII), humanitarian intervention (the use of all necessary means to establish a secure environment for humanitarian relief operations), and peacekeeping (referring to a future transition to a Chapter VI peacekeeping operation).

In addition, the command and control relationship between the United Nations and the United States was, to say the least, unusual. UNITAF was under U.S. command and operational control, under General Robert Johnston; the UN largely stood aside from the management, command and control of the operation. There was some co-ordination between UNITAF and UNOSOM I. A small UNOSOM I liaison cell was established at UNITAF headquarters, and General Johnston and the U.S. special envoy, Ambassador Robert Oakley, consulted with UNOSOM I Commander General Imtiaz Shaheen and the Secretary-General's Special Representative to Somalia, Ambassador Ismat Kittani. A high-level policy group and an operational task force were also formed at UN headquarters in New York to communicate with Washington, and a unit in the Department of Peacekeeping Operations was formed to maintain contact with UNOSOM I.

UNITAF: A Troubled Mission. On 9 December 1992, UNITAF, also under the U.S. code name Operation Restore Hope, began operations by seizing the port and airfield in Mogadishu. Progress was impressive, made possible by the massive deployment of U.S. personnel and materiel. By 28 December, UNITAF contingents had established operations in eight Humanitarian Relief Sectors.[24] At its height, UNITAF deployed 37,000 personnel (8,000 at sea). The operation was largely successful in creating a higher level of security for humanitarian workers. Distribution points and supply routes were opened and secured, the flow of aid increased, and relief efforts could be conducted over the central and southern parts of the country.

The peace process also began to bear fruit; a meeting of Somalia's factions in Addis Ababa led to a general ceasefire agreement on 8 January

1993 and a supplementary agreement seven days later. However, UNITAF soon encountered some serious disputes over mission tasks between UN officials (including the Secretary-General) and UNITAF commanders.

The first dispute concerned the coverage of UNITAF. The position of the U.S. government was that UNITAF would devote its greatest efforts to regions in greatest need; UNITAF's responsibility would not extend over the entire country. However, unsatisfactory conditions persisted in areas where UNITAF did not operate, and Boutros-Ghali argued that UNITAF ought to extend its operations to cover the entire country. This was never achieved; UNITAF never extended its control to more than 40 per cent of the country.

The second dispute concerned the national reconstruction mission. On 8 December, Boutros-Ghali declared that UNITAF would "prepare the way for political, economic, and social reconstruction" and that the UN intended "to restore the hope of the Somali people."[25] This provision was not included in the original UNITAF mission statement. The U.S. government was not enthusiastic about either a national reconstruction role for UNITAF or any involvement in the political reconciliation process; UNITAF's mission was to secure the environment for humanitarian relief supplies.[26]

A third dispute revolved around the issue of disarmament of Somalia's factions. Although Resolution 794 did not refer to disarmament, Boutros-Ghali argued that this had to be a central part of the mission, both to secure the environment and to facilitate the operations of UNOSOM II and UN efforts at national reconciliation and reconstruction.[27] However, the United States did not accept that disarmament was one of UNITAF's central missions and maintained that the task entailed both a level of risk and a longer-term commitment that were inconsistent with U.S. policy.

UNITAF was deployed with this dispute unresolved.[28] However, the Addis Ababa agreements of 8 and 15 January provided for the disarmament of the militias and the cantonment of their weapons. This process was conducted jointly by UNITAF and UNOSOM personnel and Somali representatives. These arrangements were voluntary, and no formal, uniform modalities were put in place. UNITAF therefore had a disarmament mission, but it was dependent on Somali co-operation. Where such co-operation was lacking, the U.S. view was that a comprehensive, coercive disarmament policy was not part of UNITAF's mission. As a result, while some local disarmament did take place under UNITAF, no coherent coercive disarmament policy was implemented.[29] Contingents from the United Arab Emirates and Saudi Arabia also refused to take part in the coercive disarmament of Somalia's warring clans.

These disputes reflected the efforts of the Secretary-General to change the parameters of a mission that had not been entirely agreed upon and over which the United Nations had no control. The Secretary-General and the UN had a set of objectives and goals in Somalia; however, not all were shared by UNITAF, the principal intervention instrument in Somalia for five months. On 4 May 1993, consistent with the conception of UNITAF as a short-term operation, UNITAF turned over command and operational control to UNOSOM II. U.S. operations in Somalia were turned over to Operation Continue Hope and a quick reaction force that remained in the region to support UNOSOM II.

The Transition to UNOSOM II. The genesis of UNOSOM II was twofold. First, UNITAF was designed as a short-term operation, and a follow-on UN presence was required once UNITAF operations ceased. Second, while UNITAF did improve conditions for relief efforts substantially, a secure environment was never fully established — and not established at all in the north-east, the north-west, or along the Somali/Kenyan border. The establishment of UNOSOM II was a complex undertaking, for UNOSOM II was not an entirely new operation, but rather involved expanding the size and altering the mandate of UNOSOM I. In addition, a smooth transition from UNITAF to UNOSOM II had to be effected, as the new mission was adopting many of the tasks of UNITAF, and many national contingents in UNITAF were to come under UNOSOM II's operational control.[30]

UNOSOM II was created by UN Security Council Resolution 814 on 26 March 1993. It was the first UN operation of its kind mounted under Chapter VII of the UN Charter and was derived from Boutros-Ghali's peace enforcement concept as outlined in *Agenda for Peace*. With an authorized strength of 28,000 personnel, including 8,000 logistics personnel, and at a projected cost of $1.55 billion U.S., UNOSOM II would attempt to complete the task begun by UNITAF to restore peace, stability, and law and order.[31] Operations would extend over the entire country, and mission tasks included maintaining security in a volatile environment, disarming the factions and irregulars, and assisting with mine clearance, refugee repatriation, and the establishment of a police force. UNOSOM II would also embark on peacebuilding or national reconstruction, although its Chapter VII powers would not extend to Somalia's political process. In the Secretary-General's report to the Security Council on 3 March 1992, Boutros-Ghali urged that UNOSOM II assist the Somali people in "rebuilding their shattered economy and social and political life, re-establishing the country's institutional structure, achieving national political reconciliation, recreating a Somali state based on democratic governance and rehabilitating the country's economy and infrastructure."[32] As the first UNOSOM II commander Cevik Bir attested, "We are here to re-establish a nation."[33]

UNOSOM II and the National Reconciliation Process. In March 1993, representatives of Somalia's warring factions met again at Addis Ababa at a UN-sponsored conference. On 27 March, these representatives signed a framework document intended to establish the foundation for political reconciliation and a new Somali government.[34] The UN-sponsored agreement was designed through a complex system of representation to ensure that the factions would not dominate a transitional national council (TNC). There were restrictions on the number of representatives the factions could appoint to the TNC, a quota of seats was reserved for women, and district councils were to be popularly elected. When the UN-sponsored conference closed on 27 March, however, the Somali factions continued to negotiate and, three days later, signed a document with a very different vision of representation on the TNC. Restrictions on the number of representatives appointed by the factional leaders were lifted, and there was no mention of a quota for women. A timetable in the agreement left insufficient time to organize genuinely popular elections for district councils.[35] UNOSOM II never recognized the 30 March agreement. There was therefore a split between UNOSOM II and the factional leaders on what the framework for national reconciliation actually was.

Another dispute centred around judicial and police appointments. UNOSOM II officials (in violation of the 27 March Addis Ababa agreement) reserved the power to nominate some judges for a reconstituted Somali judiciary and declared the 1962 Somali Penal Code as the law in force in Somalia. Somali factions (in particular the USC and the SNA) were bitterly resentful of what they perceived was a circumvention of their authority on these matters. As a result of these disputes, the conditions were in place for a confrontation between UNOSOM II and Somali factions.

The Growing Dispute Between General Aideed and UNOSOM II. After the Addis Ababa conferences, General Aideed attempted to organize a peace conference for central Somalia under his chairmanship and agenda, and with UNOSOM II co-operation and support. UNOSOM II sought to broaden the conference and have it chaired not by Aideed but by a former president of the Somali Republic, Alman Abdullah Osman. There was also a dispute about the agenda, with General Aideed insisting that only issues of relevance to central Somalia be included. UNOSOM II withdrew its support from the conference, and General Aideed proceeded to convene the conference on his own. This incident triggered the aggressive anti-UNOSOM and anti-foreigner rhetoric of the SNA-controlled Radio Mogadishu, which referred to UNOSOM II as an aggressive and colonizing force. This propaganda, coupled with concerns that possession of Radio Mogadishu constituted a potentially decisive advantage for Aideed in central Somalian politics, made the radio station another subject of tension between UNOSOM II and General Aideed.[36] Silencing Radio Mogadishu became an issue in UNOSOM II. It was decided that, as the station buildings had been designated by the SNA as one of five weapons storage sites in southern Mogadishu (and was therefore subject to inspection), an inspection would be carried out — and at the same time information about the station could be obtained.

The Armed Clash between UNOSOM II and General Aideed. The Pakistani UNOSOM II inspection teams arrived at the weapons storage sites in southern Mogadishu on the morning of 5 June 1993. After it had carried out the inspection of the Radio Station, the contingent was fired upon, and in the ensuing battle between SNA militia and supporters and Pakistani troops, 23 Pakistani soldiers were killed. This precipitated Security Council Resolution 837 the next day, reaffirming the right of UNOSOM II personnel to use "all necessary measures against those responsible for the armed attacks."[37] For the next four months, UNOSOM II battled Aideed's forces in a virtual war in Mogadishu.[38]

As the violence escalated, U.S. army rangers (dispatched by the United States to Somalia to capture General Aideed and other SNA officials) began to conduct operations in Mogadishu independent of UNOSOM II. On 3 October, 18 U.S. army rangers were killed and 75 wounded in an effort to capture General Aideed. Their bodies were mistreated, and video tapes of this mistreatment were played on U.S. television. Although the mission was under U.S. command and operational control, the UNOSOM-operated rescue mission came under heavy criticism.[39] In the aftermath of this incident, the Clinton administration reinforced U.S. forces with a joint task force and announced its intention to withdraw its forces from Somalia by 31 March 1994. The experience in Somalia also prompted the Clinton administration to distance itself from peacekeeping in presidential decision directive 25 (PDD-25) and to shun involvement in Rwanda.[40]

These incidents, together with deterioration of the security situation in Somalia, announcements from the Swedish, Belgian and French governments that they would withdraw their contingents, and, above all, the persistent failure of the national reconciliation effort, began to take their toll.[41] In his November 1993 report to the Security Council, the Secretary-General raised the possibility of reducing the size and mandate of UNOSOM II.[42] On 4 February 1994, in Resolution 897, the Security Council authorized the reduction of UNOSOM II to 22,000 personnel, as well as preparations to enable the force to "discharge its responsibilities."[43] By November, the Security Council had extended the mandate of UNOSOM for a final period to 31 March 1995 and directed the withdrawal of UNOSOM personnel "as soon as possible."[44] On 3 March 1995, the last UNOSOM II personnel were withdrawn from Somalia.[45]

Despite the alleviation of famine conditions, the political and security dimension of the UN effort in Somalia can only be described as a failure. On the departure of the last units of UNOSOM II, the political factions were no nearer to a settlement; since then, fighting between clan and sub-clan factions has continued and banditry has resumed. There is little semblance of governance except at the informal and local level, and services and infrastructure have largely fallen into disrepair. Somalia has left the world stage, but in little better condition for recovery from the collapse of 1990-91.

Somalia as an Example of Peace Enforcement

The UN experience in Somalia provides an excellent example of the qualities and character (as well as some of the problems) of peace enforcement operations discussed in Chapter 3:

- UNOSOM I, UNITAF, and UNOSOM II were conducted entirely within the territorial boundaries of Somalia.
- There was no central government to negotiate with.
- Consent was subject to negotiation among many factions and subject to failures to comply with agreements. The principle of consent was increasingly abandoned by the UN, even before the creation of UNITAF under Chapter VII of the Charter.
- UN peacekeepers were operating in a hostile environment, where they were subject to obstruction, threats, invective, and armed attacks.
- UNOSOM II was a large operation, with an authorized strength of 28,000 personnel.

- UNITAF and UNOSOM II personnel were heavily armed and used high levels of force, particularly in the struggle against General Aideed. The UN became involved in a virtual shooting war in Mogadishu.
- There were uncertainties, misunderstandings and disagreements about mission mandates and tasks within the UN effort and between the UN and UNITAF.
- The UN was marginalized by the U.S.-led UNITAF operation, then had to move quickly to create a follow-on mission to UNITAF.
- The UN mission in Somalia was multifunctional, involving a wide variety of tasks, from providing security for humanitarian relief to disarmament to infrastructure repair.
- UNOSOM II had a peacebuilding or national reconstruction component.
- Media coverage played a significant role during the crisis and had a direct impact on the missions, particularly UNITAF and UNOSOM II.

THE LESSONS OF SOMALIA

The Importance of a Post-Mortem on Somalia

The Somalia experience was a traumatic one for the United Nations and a blow to the vision of Secretary-General Boutros Boutros-Ghali as expressed in *Agenda for Peace*. Not only did the experience in Somalia end in a most unsatisfactory manner, but it came at a time when the UN was struggling with the troubles afflicting its other high-profile missions in Cambodia and Yugoslavia.[46] The difficulties encountered by the UN in the conduct of the big three peace operations — UNPROFOR, UNTAC, and UNOSOM II — all contributed to a growing perception that the UN was unsuited and ill-equipped to mount operations of such scope, ambition, and magnitude successfully. It remains to be seen whether this experience caused long-term damage to the ability of the UN to act as an instrument of conflict management. It is for this reason that identifying the implications and lessons of the effort in Somalia is so important. This is not just an academic exercise, for an assessment of the lessons of Somalia, however belated, can contribute to the future efficacy of UN peace operations. Just as traditional peacekeeping during the Cold War developed out of a conceptual vacuum over time and in light of experience, future peace operations will evolve and develop a conceptual base suited to new conditions and tasks. However, this may prove difficult, for it is easier to build on success than on failure, and it is easier to expand one's ambitions and goals than contract them.

The Potential Contradiction in the Concept of Peacemaking

Use of Force Can Undermine Legitimacy. The fundamental contradiction in the concept of the peace enforcement operation in Somalia lies in the enhanced role of force and coercion, which is explicit in UN operations of the kind conducted in Somalia. Can a lasting peace and achievement of national reconciliation (or even tactical arrangements such as ceasefires and opening of transport routes) be achieved by the same agency that has used military force or the threat of force to encourage the parties to a conflict to come to the negotiating table? As one UN official put it, "The lesson of Somalia may have been that you can't impose peace."[47]

In traditional peacekeeping operations, UN contingents rely heavily on popular and elite perceptions of the legitimacy of the mission as a whole and of the civilian and military personnel performing mission tasks. Legitimacy, in turn, depends on perceptions of the impartiality of the force, the permission extended for its presence, and its non-coercive nature. If this legitimacy is lost, the peacekeeping operation loses the basis of its presence and its effectiveness. However, in peace enforcement operations, UN contingents have relied more heavily on a credible capacity to use force to coerce or compel warring factions toward a settlement, punish ceasefire violators, disarm factions, deliver humanitarian relief supplies, or protect refugee sites and safe zones. The problem — and the contradiction — is that in the absence of a coherent and established political plan, the greater use of force by UN contingents undercuts the basis of the UN's presence and its peace and negotiation efforts designed to build such a plan. The loss of impartiality, presence without consent, and a coercive role do not constitute a solid foundation for arbiter, mediation, or third-party roles. The success of traditional UN PKOs does not necessarily lie with the big battalions. Military force, even a preponderance of force, does not necessarily make for effective peacekeeping or peacemaking. On the contrary, the application of such force can be a fundamental misapplication of means to ends if it is not conducted in a discriminate and proportional manner in support of a political framework. In the effort to apply the principles of traditional peacekeeping to a very different environment that involved greater use of force, the UN created a self-contradictory hybrid operation, which was neither a traditional peacekeeping operation nor a collective security enforcement action. The United Nations could not operate in Somalia under traditional peacekeeping precepts, but it was not willing to abandon the country either. The UN was unwilling to tolerate obstructions from local factions, but it was also unwilling to forsake those factions and exert firm control over the country. Instead, the UN attempted to operate in a grey area between peace-keeping and collective security enforcement, seeking to use some of the elements of both.

Significance of the Loss of Impartiality and Consent. Impartiality and consent are the bedrock of the distinction between UN contingents and the parties to a conflict.[48] If these are lost, the UN contingent will come to be seen as another actor in a continuing conflict, another potential or real adversary for the parties to a conflict to account for in their political and military calculations. In a fragmented political situation of the kind that existed in Somalia, the impartiality of a mission (or the perception of impartiality) is particularly vulnerable if force is misapplied as an instrument of the UN's aims.

First, actions (or inactions) can easily be regarded by one or more factions as an example of UN favouritism or bias. Second, when attempts are made to intimidate, coerce, compel, or punish, the UN mission in effect resigns its impartial aspect and becomes a participant in the conflict. Once this has occurred, it is difficult, if not impossible, to re-establish an impartial posture. Efforts against General Aideed rallied some clans and sub-clans to Aideed, while others that opposed Aideed supported the UN. UNOSOM II had, in effect, generated a new alliance pattern and had become a component in the shifting alliances of the Somali factions. Third, efforts to intimidate, coerce, compel, or punish can provoke latent anti-foreigner sentiment. In a country with a history of fierce independence and resistance to foreign rule, many Somalis came to regard UNITAF and UNOSOM II as a foreign power. Impartiality can hardly be sustained in the face of such perceptions, yet the UN continued to operate as if it had maintained this impartiality.

Lessons of the Application of Force. The implications of any resort to force by UN contingents, or any mandate to use force to achieve mission objectives, should be clear. Nevertheless, contingencies in which force will be used are sure to arise. The way force is applied will be crucial to success in such contingencies:

- Force can be counter-productive if it is not used in support of an established, coherent political plan.
- Firepower, and the use of lethal force, should not be applied at long range by stand-off weapons platforms (artillery, aircraft, helicopters)

in built-up areas, for this largely indiscriminate, arbitrary form of coercion is most likely to turn the sentiments of the local population against the UN contingent.
- Firepower is a poor force multiplier in peacekeeping or peace enforcement operations. If force must be applied, it should be conducted against specific targets using a minimum of force.
- In peacekeeping or peace enforcement operations, intelligence and information are the most important force multipliers.
- Presence on the ground in the form of well equipped, mobile personnel able to operate at night and in poor weather can have a greater deterrent or coercive impact than the application of firepower.
- Restraint and discipline are critical at the tactical level, whatever the mandate and rules of engagement.

The Creation of a 'Somalia Syndrome'

The Somalia Syndrome and the Mogadishu Line. The experience in Vietnam had a number of consequences for future U.S. decision making on security and military affairs. These consequences, sometimes referred to collectively as the Vietnam Syndrome, included a confused legal relationship between branches of the U.S. government with respect to war-making powers; hesitancy about future involvement in insurgency conflict, especially in Asia; loss of public support for the military, the use of force, and the government's foreign policy powers; and a military psychology favouring the use of overwhelming force with minimal political interference.

Similarly, the UN operation in Somalia has had a number of consequences that, though different from those experienced by the United States after Vietnam, have the potential to influence the future of UN peace operations. Foremost among these was a belief (led by the United States) that the UN could not solve all the world's problems and had to learn when to say no to new missions. Somalia also instilled a reluctance to get involved in subsequent contingencies with a similar geographic or political context. The experience in Somalia was a significant factor in the failure of the UN and its membership to react swiftly and forcefully in Rwanda and Burundi. The Somalia experience also prompted many member states — most prominently the United States but traditional troop contributors as well — to reappraise their involvement in UN peace operations and to adopt more cautious policies on involvement. The purpose of such caution has been to ensure that governments do not become entangled in UN operations of high risk and uncertain duration and with low probabilities of success. Governments now fear crossing the 'Mogadishu line' in terms of using force in UN operations. Another negative consequence is the lack of confidence in the UN's decision-making process, its ability to manage large operations, and the perception of interference by UN officials in the conduct of military operations. The Somalia Syndrome has arisen from the consequences of two phenomena experienced by participants in the UN effort: mandate escalation and mission creep.

Mandate Escalation and Mission Creep. UN involvement in Somalia was characterized by ever-increasing levels of engagement recommended by the Secretary-General and supported by the Security Council. From an initial involvement in the negotiations between Somalia's warring factions, the UN embarked on a small peacekeeping force (which was subsequently expanded in mandate if not in fact), then turned to Chapter VII operations under UNITAF and UNOSOM II. The catalyst was the failure or inapplicability of traditional instruments — ceasefires, demarcation lines, separation of factions — to achieve UN goals. As a result, the UN sought increasingly to use force to achieve its objectives. However, the use of force compromised and undermined the viability of the mission by undercutting impartiality and making the UN a combatant in the dispute.

At every stage in the escalation of UN involvement, the size, expense, and intended tasks of the mission expanded, with new mandates piled on top of previous ones with little coherence. As one study has argued, "Evaluation of UNOSOM at all levels has concluded that the operation's mandate was vague, changed frequently during the process and was open to myriad interpretations."[49]

In the absence of a coherent political plan, the military mission dominated. Each escalation of the UN's involvement was an effort to respond to the failures of the previous level of engagement, primarily over security for relief supplies, the integrity of ceasefires, and the national reconciliation process. Each effort deepened the UN commitment and increased the stakes of success in Somalia. Even at the highest levels of its capacity, the UN could not achieve its goals in the country, and it had neither a political nor a military fallback position. Contraction or withdrawal were not seen as options until the mission began to implode when key contingents were withdrawn by their governments as the prospects for success became increasingly dim.

UN involvement in Somalia was also characterized by mission creep, the incremental expansion of mission tasks from an original, limited concept of operations. UN contingents deployed initially under certain conventions of conduct and rules of engagement soon found themselves operating with very different ones. Tasks such as disarmament, detention, and national reconstruction were often handed down to UN contingents after their deployment under mission profiles that did not include such tasks. Dissension was rife among UN contingents; France followed the instructions of its national government, while Italy ran a policy largely independent and sometimes at odds with that of the UN.

Negative Consequences of Mandate Escalation and Mission Creep. Mandate escalation and mission creep have a number of negative consequences for peacekeeping missions, including the following:

- They can create a gap between the tasks and missions assigned to a UN operation and the forces and resources available to carry out those tasks, with a consequent increase in risk to personnel.
- They can lead to friction among UN contingents and their national governments, as disputes arise over the tasks of the UN mission, their appropriateness to the mission, or the refusal of some contingents to perform tasks not previously agreed to or anticipated.
- They can place great pressure on the flexibility, resourcefulness, training, and experience of UN contingents, some of which will be more capable of adapting than others, thus widening the degree of inconsistent quality across the national contingents in the force.
- They can drag the UN deeper into conflicts from which it cannot easily disengage.
- They can promote hesitancy among national governments in responding to future UN requests for contributions until very specific criteria or conditions are satisfied, or unless they have increased or complete control over the conduct of operations.
- Finally, they can create opposition to mandates that permit the use of force in situations that might in fact be manageable by the careful application of force.

In the future, these problems can be reduced if the UN (and particularly engaged member states) takes steps to ensure that:

- mission mandates are crafted with greater clarity and reduce or eliminate divergences between member states at the outset;
- stronger links are established between mission objectives and mission tasks;

- co-ordinated, integrated political plans are established that are matched to available military and civilian resources.

The Need to Establish Mechanisms for Dealing with Statelessness

Statelessness. The UN effort in Somalia illustrates the need for modalities of conduct in situations where the state is for all intents and purposes absent as a coherent entity — little or no central government, no operational services, no administrative capacity, no police, and no armed forces. However, the UN, most NGOs, and states are designed or conceptually equipped to operate with the structures of a state. Governance in Somalia was, and is, conducted at the local level and is characterized by fluid and flexible arrangements between parties with no clear lines of hierarchical authority or formality. The UN, its agencies, NGOs, and other states must learn to operate where there is no equivalent structure to plug into or interact with. This situation can be aggravated by the fact that statelessness has its advocates — those who profit from the lack of a centralized authority. These may be racketeers or smugglers, political factions, elders or religious leaders, bandits, or the victors of past battles who stand to lose territory, resources, or power if a central authority is established. There are, of course, centralizing forces, such as coalitions and commercial interests, that may profit from the establishment of a central authority.

In its efforts to establish such an authority, the UN can expect resistance from some elements and the support of others, a situation that again can compromise impartiality. As noted by Chopra and Nordbo, "Peacekeeping between factions in internal conflicts can further fragment a collapsed state."[50] The UN lacks individuals trained and/or experienced in establishing the foundations of order in anarchic conditions such as those encountered in Somalia. The UN has limited (though growing) experience in the administration of public institutions and services, police forces, judiciary, elections, and co-ordination with aid agencies on cultivation and livestock replenishment. The UN also lacks the expertise on the deep cultural, language, religious, clan, or political nuances that are so vital to operating in an environment where the familiar, ordering influence of state structures is absent.

Operating in a Stateless Environment. The Somalia experience suggests that if the UN is to operate successfully in stateless environments in the future, it will require a number of changes in the way it conducts itself:

- an ability to be flexible and have a wide range of capabilities, expertise, and resources (military and civilian) available at the immediate local level to meet local concerns and requirements;
- decentralization of administrative and operational authority to local areas of responsibility to respond to broadly divergent local conditions, while enhancing mechanisms for feedback and oversight;
- a regional, rather than country-wide, approach to reconciliation and the establishment of peace;
- an effort to assist, rather than replace or restructure, existing systems of authority, security, or diplomacy;
- improved capacity for dealing with incidents/individuals acting outside political control (banditry, looting, rioting, individuals acting under influence of stimulants and other psychotropics);
- the accumulation and dissemination to all ranks of as much information as possible on local authorities and personalities, traditions and culture, and political, ethnic, religious cleavages and grievances; and
- an improved capability to disseminate information to locals on mission aims and activities. UN operations require a public information strategy and public information resources, such as a press and radio station. In Somalia, the budgetary committee of the General Assembly rejected the establishment of a UNOSOM radio station.[51]

The Decisive Role of the United States

The United States and the Peacekeeping/Peace Enforcement Enterprise. One of the implications of the erosion of UN operational control over peacekeeping and peace enforcement discussed in Chapter 3 was the increased potential for U.S. dominance over UN operations. The concern is that should UN operations continue on a more aggressive, intrusive, and militarized course, the United States will dominate such operations, as it is one of a very few countries with the heavy military forces and logistics capacity needed to carry out such operations. Even as the success of such operations may depend increasingly on U.S. involvement, to say nothing of general political support, the willingness of the United States to become engaged will depend on the extent to which its conditions (usually in the form of increased control over operations and missions) are met and its national interests satisfied.[52] The danger is that the UN could become a provider of political or moral sanction to U.S. policy, capable of acting only when there is a convergence of U.S. and UN interests.

Such a convergence occurred in Somalia; the UN became increasingly frustrated with the failure of the peace process, interference with humanitarian aid, and the powerlessness of UNOSOM I to do anything about it, while the Bush administration wanted to respond to a situation that posed a challenge to U.S. leadership in a post-Cold War world order. However, Operation Restore Hope was mounted only after the United States had made it clear that it would not place troops under UN command. There was also a convergence of interest on the creation of UNOSOM II. The United States had no desire to maintain large forces in Somalia, and the UN wished to ensure that UNOSOM II would receive U.S. logistical and firepower support. The withdrawal of UNITAF, and the continued presence of the United States under UNOSOM II, suited both the UN and the Clinton administration. UNOSOM II was consistent with Boutros-Ghali's desire to establish a more assertive and proactive role for the UN in peace operations. The Clinton administration saw UNOSOM II as an example of "assertive multilateralism" and a new principle of co-operation between the United States and the United Nations.

The United States and the Conduct of UN Operations. The experience in Somalia also illustrates the danger of UN operations becoming subject to shifts and turns in U.S. policy. The effort to punish General Aideed was mounted after the June 5th attack on UN forces in which 24 Pakistani peacekeepers were killed. Resolution 837 was actively pushed for by the United States. However, after a series of failed attempts to apprehend Aideed, this aim was de-emphasized by the United States, even to the point of bringing Aideed back into the political process while the UN was still bound by Resolution 837 to capture Aideed. After a series of aggressive U.S. operations, on September 28 the United States informed the UN that U.S. combat troops of the quick reaction force and ranger units were not to be used for patrols in Mogadishu. The United States then decided to strengthen its force with tanks and MICVs. There was also the long-running dispute between the UN and the United States over goals. For the UN and for Boutros Boutros-Ghali, the operation was a project in state building; for the United States, it was a humanitarian exercise.

When the United States is heavily engaged in UN missions, UN operations will be subject to the ebb and flow of U.S. policy making. Reliance on the United States also creates a problem of sustaining UN operations should the United States withdraw. A backlash has taken shape over this matter, both within the United States — in the form of shifts in public opinion and in Congress, which has attempted to exert greater control over the administration's peacekeeping policy — and outside the United States, in the form of international complaints about U.S. dominance of UN operations from Desert Storm to Restore Hope and French opposition to U.S.-led NATO peacekeeping planning.

CHAPTER SUMMARY

1. The conflict in Somalia was the result of the collapse of the state, a period of severe drought, and incessant warfare between Somalia's clans, the defining characteristic of Somali society. Somalia was not strictly speaking an ethnic or religious conflict, but a factional one.
2. UN involvement in Somalia was characterized by a process of escalating involvement in an effort to deliver humanitarian relief supplies, facilitate or compel a national reconciliation agreement, and engage in national reconstruction. Under UNITAF and UNOSOM II, UN operations were conducted under Chapter VII of the Charter, the first use of such provisions for peacekeeping.
3. Despite the virtual elimination of famine and good works performed by UN contingents at the local level, the UN departed Somalia with the factions no closer to a national reconciliation agreement, the countryside still subject to banditry, and with little national infrastructure and no government. Judged by its own measures of success, the UN effort in Somalia was a failure.
4. From the UN experience in Somalia, the following specific lessons can be drawn:

    - The UN operation in Somalia, in conjunction with the experience in Cambodia and Yugoslavia, has likely led to long-term damage to international confidence in future UN operations.
    - Force was misapplied in Somalia. Force was used in a manner that undercut the foundation of the UN's presence; it was not applied in a discriminating and calibrated fashion in support of a coherent and established political framework.
    - A Somalia Syndrome may have been created, which will hamstring UN efforts to act and may prevent appropriate UN engagement in such conflicts in the future.
    - The phenomenon of statelessness (the absence of state authority and structures) places great demands on UN operations. The UN

is not as yet well equipped to deal with the unique demands of operating in a stateless environment.
- The Somalia experience revealed the dangers inherent in heavy U.S. involvement in UN peacekeeping operations.

CHAPTER FIVE

Peacemaking, the Somalia Experience, and Canada

THE ROLE OF PEACEKEEPING IN CANADIAN SECURITY POLICY

Peacekeeping and Canadian Interests

Canada and the Genesis of Peacekeeping. Canada has a long and proud tradition of involvement in peacekeeping operations. Official Canadian literature rarely fails to remind the reader that Canada is the only country to have participated in virtually every UN peacekeeping operation since the establishment of the United Nations Truce Supervision Organization (UNTSO) on 11 June 1948 (although Canada was not a participant in UNTSO at its inception). In addition, Canada claims a special role in the development of the peacekeeping concept; it was Lester B. Pearson, then secretary of state for external affairs, who recommended the formation and deployment of a multilateral international peace and police force, subsequently named the First United Nations Emergency Force (UNEF 1), for deployment to the Suez in 1956. The force was commanded by a Canadian, Major-General E.L.M. (Tommy) Burns, who was also the serving chief of staff at UNTSO.

Despite this early commitment to the UN, there was some hesitancy about Canadian participation in UN operations (the term 'peacekeeping' was not coined until 1956). There were concerns that participation in such operations would be a drain on Canadian resources and would lead to Canada's involvement in overseas wars.

Canada's initial involvement came with the UN Military Observer Group in India and Pakistan (UNMOGIP), established on 24 January 1949. This participation was not enthusiastic; only the persistence of Lester Pearson led to the deployment of four reserve officers. Since this early beginning as a "once-reluctant peacekeeper",[1] the awarding of the Nobel Peace Prize to Pearson, the apparent success of early missions, the role peacekeeping offered Canada, and the enthusiasm displayed by the public have made peacekeeping an important component of Canadian foreign and defence policy.[2]

Peacekeeping: The Strategic Interest. Peacekeeping was far from a peripheral component of Canadian security policy. In fact, it came to fill a rather important niche in Canada's conception of its Cold War security interests. Canada's paramount strategic concern during the Cold War was that an outbreak of hostilities in Europe or elsewhere could escalate to a superpower confrontation that would threaten Canada's core interests or Canadian territory. Ultimately, any full-scale war between the superpowers would leave Canada (which was part of the North American target set) either a direct target of attack or at best a victim of severe collateral damage. Therefore, it was in Canada's interests to participate in the collective defence of Europe and the defence of North America to help deter a general European war and any attack against the continental United States. As it became evident that the United States and the Soviet Union could clash in various regional conflicts, Canada acquired an interest in the prevention, control, or containment of hostilities in areas of tension around the world, hostilities that could widen to include a superpower confrontation.[3] Peacekeeping in regions around the world contributed to Canadian security, to the extent it contributed to preventing the expansion and intensification of regional conflicts. For Canada, international security and national security became intertwined. In 1986, a Special Joint Committee of the Senate and House of Commons assumed that "the threat to Canada is one and the same with the threat to international stability and peace."[4]

Peacekeeping: The Foreign Policy Interest. Canada's foreign policy internationalism was also tied closely to concerns about Canadian sovereignty and independence and Canada's international profile. Maintaining international commitments and responsibilities, it was hoped, would act as a counterweight to the political and economic influence of the United States as well as a more general expression of Canada's claim to be acting as an independent, sovereign political entity. Peacekeeping was a leading component of this effort to chart an independent course and formed one of the cornerstones of the middle-power conception of Canada's place and role in international affairs.[5] Active diplomatic, economic, and military engagement around the world became a maxim as well as a source of pride for the Canadian political establishment and was widely accepted by Canadians.

Peacekeeping also supported another cornerstone of Canadian foreign policy: support for multilateralism and international institutions in general and service to the United Nations in particular. As a middle power, Canada relied on a co-operative approach to its security agenda, and as a country dependent on exports for its economic health, Canada relied on an open and stable international trading order. Both were served by international co-operation, institutions, and regimes, so Canadian support for such multilateral organizations and practices was an investment in Canadian security. Canada also sought to secure some international leverage or influence through peacekeeping. By contributing contingents to multilateral ventures such as peacekeeping (as well as NATO) Canada hoped to gain a seat at the table, a voice, or some input to decision making at the organizational level. The extent of this return on Canada's relatively small alliance and peacekeeping investments is uncertain and difficult to quantify, although it became an important rationale for Canadian multilateralism.[6] Finally, on occasion, specific UN peacekeeping missions also served specific Canadian interests; the UNEF 1 mission prevented a deepening of a diplomatic rift between Washington and London and Paris, and the UN operation in Cyprus (UNFICYP) helped avoid an escalation of the conflict between two of Canada's NATO allies.

The Peacekeeping Consensus. In the context of this foreign and defence policy outlook, peacekeeping became a central component in domestic conceptions of Canada's security strategy and its self-perceived international role. Peacekeeping became a highly visible and widely supported activity within Canada, as it carried a positive and moral imperative that appealed to idealistic and altruistic sentiments. Indeed, within Canada peacekeeping became associated with Canada's identity and distinctiveness on the world stage, as well as an important difference between Canada and the United States on that stage. Peacekeeping also became associated with the functions of the Canadian Armed Forces. The missions assigned to the Canadian Forces reflected the entire structure of Canadian Cold War interests; the Canadian forces were committed to collective defence in Europe, continental defence and sovereignty enforcement tasks, and peacekeeping. However, the peacekeeping mission became more visible to the public than any other form of Canadian military activity. Peacekeeping was regarded as an activity in which the armed forces could make a meaningful contribution to international peace and security. Peacekeeping featured conspicuously in government defence statements, and in military recruitment literature the blue beret was displayed prominently and proudly. This in turn raised the profile of the peacekeeping mission in Canada, the association of the armed forces with peacekeeping, and the good will of Canadians toward UN conflict management efforts.

The Dark Side: The Worsening Commitment/Capability Gap. One of the enduring characteristics of Cold War Canadian security policy was a persistent gap between commitment and capability. Throughout the Cold War, successive Canadian governments maintained security commitments to Europe and NATO, to North American Defence and NORAD, to defence of the Atlantic sea lanes of communication and the maritime approaches to Canada, and to the UN and peacekeeping. However, expenditures on defence by those governments were not sufficient to sustain both the size of the force and the equipment required to meet those demands. The refusal of Canadian governments to scale back on commitments resulted in many compromises. The overall size of the force as well as the number of operational units were reduced steadily, outdated equipment remained in service for lack of replacements, and many operational units were committed to more than one contingency. The forces, though of high quality in terms of personnel, were overstretched in terms of the commitments they were asked to maintain. As a result, the deployment and use of the Canadian Armed Forces became largely symbolic. Canada committed a small number of troops or ships or aircraft to secure its membership in regional and multilateral organizations. These tokens or 'antes' were the small price Canada had to pay for the internationalist foreign policy it maintained.

In this context, peacekeeping was uniquely suited to Canada's capabilities as well as its interests. Peacekeeping required relatively small numbers of highly trained, high-quality personnel, armed primarily with light weapons. However, with the surge in UN peacekeeping operations that began in 1989, coupled with downward pressure on the defence budget after the end of the Cold War, the commitment/capability gap worsened. Even the withdrawal of Canada's forces stationed in Germany and the termination of the commitment to the UN operation in Cyprus could not offer more than temporary relief from the demands placed on the shrinking armed forces. It was in this context that Canada became engaged in UN operations in the former Yugoslavia and in Somalia.

PEACE ENFORCEMENT, CANADA, AND THE SOMALIA EXPERIENCE

Peace Enforcement and Canadian Interests

The End of the Cold War and Canadian Strategic Calculation. Canadians welcomed the end of the Cold War for many reasons, but mostly because it promised relief from the tensions, fears, and international crises of the previous 45 years and promised an era of peace, prosperity, and co-operation on social, environmental, and economic issues. Relief and optimism did not last long, however, as regional conflicts, disputes among allies, economic recession, and concerns about a wide variety of 'new' security issues — terrorism, the environment, weapons proliferation — emerged.

It did not take long for the implications of the collapse of the Soviet Union to sink in for Canadian security policy makers and analysts. Although the arrival of Gorbachev and the subsequent decline in the perception of the Soviet threat played a significant role in the rapid obsolescence of the 1987 White Paper on Defence and many of the Cold War strategic rationales it exonerated, the subsequent collapse of the Warsaw Pact and the Soviet Union removed the military and ideological threat to Europe and North America. For Canada, the collapse of the Soviet threat severed the link between conflict overseas — inside and outside the NATO area — and direct threats to North America and the North American target set. The focus and strategic rationale for Canadian foreign and defence policy had vanished, and no obvious alternative presented itself. In addition to removing this strategic rationale, the erosion of the Soviet threat in the late 1980s and the subsequent end of the Cold War presented a challenge to the international institutions that had played such an important role in Canadian multilateralism and the exertion of middle-power diplomacy. Unlike European countries, which could look to the restructuring of European defence and the role to be played by NATO or some incarnation of a European defence identity in the new Europe, Canada was not presented with an immediately obvious regional or issue-oriented security agenda by virtue of the end of the Cold War.

Peace Enforcement and Canadian Interests After the Cold War. Despite sea changes in the world and their profound implications for Canadian foreign and defence policy, UN peacekeeping was one Cold War role that did not immediately seem altered fundamentally by the changing strategic environment of the late 1980s. In fact, it appeared as if the relevance of peacekeeping was on the rise. Canada continued to contribute to new UN peacekeeping operations, including the larger and more ambitious efforts in Cambodia, Somalia, and the former Yugoslavia. It did so because peacekeeping retained an important place in upholding Canadian interests in the post-Cold War world. These interests included:

- Controlling or preventing the outbreak or spread of regional conflicts. After the collapse of the Soviet Union, Canada continued to define its security interests in terms of general threats to international security. As regional conflicts were now increasingly identified as threats to international peace and stability, they were, by extension, threats to this general Canadian interest. Efforts to prevent, contain, or terminate these conflicts, short of causing serious diplomatic rifts between Canadian allies, were therefore worthy of Canadian participation. Spillover and escalation of regional conflicts continued to be a Canadian concern. Canadian participation in the Gulf War, albeit grudging, was motivated at least in part by this interest.
- Maintaining the effectiveness of international institutions and regimes suited to maintaining international peace and security (and especially the UN). As Canada would continue to lack the influence to address international conflict or the reinforcement of international co-operation on its own, Canada would continue to contribute to international institutions and regimes that could do so. If international institutions were a bulwark against the erosion or collapse of international political security and economic co-operation, and were key actors in efforts to address regional conflicts, it was in Canada's interests to contribute to their efforts in every way possible, including the provision of military assets.
- Maintaining an international voice for Canada. The desire to be both represented in and consulted on international affairs continued to be an important driving force behind Canadian foreign policy. Canada would continue to pursue an internationalist foreign policy after the Cold War, and the effort to secure an international voice for Canada (and attendant expectations of some degree of influence over post-Cold War affairs) depended on continued Canadian contributions to multilateral efforts, whether these were in the form of contributions to NATO, NORAD, international coalitions such as the Gulf War, or the UN.
- Input into regional diplomacy where Canada would not otherwise have access. Peacekeeping allows Canada to engage in many of the world's regions where its presence in other political channels — alliances,

development policy, or diplomacy — is lacking, on the wane, or without a solid material foundation. Peacekeeping and peace enforcement therefore stand as tangible symbols of Canada's commitment not only to international institutions and multilateralism but to the region where Canadian contingents are deployed as well. This is particularly true in Europe, where the Canadian contribution to UN efforts in Yugoslavia has been held out as an example of Canada's commitment to European security.
- Maintaining counterweights against the political, economic, and defence predominance of the United States. The end of the Cold War did not render the counterweight concept obsolete. Canada continues to have an interest in maintaining an ability to engage in foreign and defence policy activity independent of the United States as an element attesting to Canada's national distinctiveness. Canada is still neighbour of the United States, with all that entails for political and economic autonomy and sovereignty.
- Preventing serious disruptions in the international economy. Canada's economic and physical security remained linked to an open international trading order. There is still a direct link between Canadian interests and efforts to prevent the intensification or widening of regional conflicts and the fear that such disputes could damage an environment that currently provides both open trade and physical security.[7]

It was for these reasons, or a combination of them, that Canada continued to contribute to UN peace operations in a changing global strategic context. This consistency with earlier rationales is also a function of the incremental fashion in which post-Cold War Canadian foreign and defence policy evolved. In the absence of radical rethinking, policy planners continued to operate with Cold War institutions and ideas, adapting them when possible to new contingencies and new agendas. The impact of this practical, day-to-day decision-making reality should not be forgotten in explanations of the evolution of Canadian security policy since the late 1980s. Canada was still committed to multilateralism, had high hopes for the UN, was favourably disposed toward UN conflict management efforts, and had a long and proud tradition of participating in UN peacekeeping. These interests and rationales led Canada into the Chapter VII UN operation in Somalia.

Canada and Peace Enforcement in Somalia

Getting There, Part 1: Overstretch and the Decision to Deploy the Canadian Airborne Regiment. On 28 August 1992, the government of Canada agreed to a UN request to contribute to UNOSOM. The Canadian contribution was based around the Canadian Airborne Regiment (CAR) and was code-named Operation Cordon (OP Cordon). The warning order to prepare for the mission was given to the CAR on 4 September. Between 8 September and 2 October, the CAR conducted mission-specific training for OP Cordon and was pronounced operationally ready on 13 November. The CAR was to be deployed to Bossasso in northeastern Somalia.

The CAR was selected for the Somalia mission for the following reasons:

- The CAR had been designated as Canada's UN standby battalion.
- The CAR was in an advanced state of preparedness for the mission, ready to deploy its headquarters in 7 days and follow-on elements in 30 days.
- The CAR had undergone training for a deployment to North Africa.
- Other units were available, but these required a longer preparation time of up to 90 days, and it was anticipated that these units would be required to go to Bosnia.

At this time in 1992, Canada had 2,279 personnel deployed abroad, with another 1,200 promised for the UN effort in the former Yugoslavia. This was in the context of a force reduction plan that would see the armed forces decline from 84,000 to 75,000 and regular troops decline in number from 23,000 to 18,000.[8] By November 1992, with 0.5 per cent of the world's population and the world's 100th-largest army, Canada was providing 10 per cent of UN peacekeeping forces.[9] Concerns were expressed about time diverted from training, the ability of Canada to maintain forces ready to meet other commitments, and the amount of time Canadian personnel would be able to spend back home before being deployed again, with its consequences for morale. In November, the chief of the defence staff, General John de Chastelain, warned that "The army is now at the maximum limit of its expeditionary capability for formed units."[10]

The decision to send the CAR was made under demanding circumstances. The government had committed the country to the mission, many other UN missions were under way at the time, the forces remained committed to other non-UN missions, and the availability of units was extremely low. The CAR was operationally ready and in line to deploy, and no other unit was available to deploy in the immediate time frame.

The argument that the CAR was sent to Somalia despite disciplinary problems because other units were not available cannot be made without qualification. In the first place, the extent to which the military and civilian officials responsible for the dispatch of the CAR were aware of disciplinary problems in the regiment is not clear at this time. Also unclear is to what extent knowledge of such problems should have disqualified some or all of the regiment's personnel from deployment. It is also possible that Canada could have sent another unit at some point in the future, likely beyond a 60- to 90-day time frame. However, it is nonetheless true that no other unit was immediately available for deployment at the time. Had another unit been available, there would have been an option to send such a unit instead of the CAR in light of known or rumoured disciplinary problems. In the context of the demands placed on the resources of the armed forces at the time, such an option simply was not available. Canada was at the very limit of its deployable capabilities.

Getting There, Part 2: The Canadian Deployment to Somalia. In late November 1992, there was discussion about a reinforced mission in Somalia. During a period of considerable uncertainty about the shape of this mission, preparation for OP Cordon continued, and deployment to Somalia was delayed, until it emerged that UNOSOM operations would be frozen while a U.S.-led operation was mounted. When the UN Security Council approved the establishment of UNITAF on 4 December 1992, the CAR was reassigned to the UNITAF operation, under Operation Deliverance. For this new mission, the Canadian contribution was upgraded; the CAR was augmented with a mortar platoon from the 1st battalion, Royal Canadian Regiment, and an armoured squadron from the Royal Canadian Dragoons. This force was renamed the Canadian Airborne Regiment Battlegroup (CARBG). In addition, Operation Deliverance involved naval and air elements.

The entire Canadian contribution was referred to as Canadian Joint Force Somalia (CJFS). CJFS was composed of the CARBG, a Rotary Wing Aviation Flight, Canadian Air Transport Detachment Somalia, HMCS Preserver (until March 1993), and a Field Squadron (from 1 May 1993). The headquarters of CJFS was formed from 1st Canadian Division Headquarters. The first elements of the CARBG began their deployment on 13 December 1992, with the main body of the CARBG arriving by 28 December and the bulk of the heavy equipment arriving in January. Initially assigned to airfield security at Bela Dogle[11] under the operational control of the U.S. 10th Mountain Division, the CARBG was reassigned after Canada agreed to assume responsibility for the Belet Huen Humanitarian Relief Sector (HRS), some 350 kilometres from Mogadishu.

Deployment to Belet Huen was completed on 15 January 1993. The Belet Huen sector was approximately 30,000 square kilometres in size, an unrealistically large area for a force the size of the CARBG to secure. The size of the Belet Huen HRS would challenge the mobility, logistics, and endurance of CARBG personnel throughout the mission.

Mission Tasks. While in Somalia, the CARBG performed a wide range of tasks. The general mission was to protect aid agency personnel and aid distribution points.[12] More specifically, the CARBG was to secure the supply routes in the Belet Huen HRS. This required constant patrolling throughout the operation, often at night. The CARBG also acted to prevent clashes between rival factions in the Belet Huen HRS and conducted the cantonment of major weapons. Other mission tasks included:

- technical assistance to NGOs through a civil/military co-operation unit;
- reconstitution of local constabulary and judiciary;
- mine awareness training;
- assistance to reconstitute schools;
- transport of relief supplies;
- construction of a Bailey bridge; and
- road and runway repair.

Many of these mission tasks were little different from tasks performed in earlier traditional peacekeeping operations.

Explaining the Belet Huen Incidents: Permissive, Necessary, Sufficient, and Efficient Causes. It is unfortunate that the Canadian operation in Somalia is better known within Canada for the misconduct of a small number of the members of the CARBG than it is for the activities just listed. The incidents of misconduct include the beating death of a Somali national by 2 Commando personnel and the shooting death and wounding of two other Somali nationals. These incidents, combined with the public release of video tapes of CAR personnel in unauthorized hazing activities and uttering racial slurs, led to disbanding the CAR.

The explanations for these incidents are many and varied, but they fall generally into one of three alternative conceptions. The first is an individual explanation, which regards the incidents as the result of the racism and misconduct of a very few individuals within the CAR. A second explanation focuses on a group analysis and finds the explanation in the culture of the CAR or the commandos, a culture that emphasized group loyalty, tolerated racism and indiscipline, and erected a wall of silence against efforts to investigate the group. A third explanation emphasizes the broader structural context and the impact this might have had on creating the conditions in which the incidents took place.

Each explanation suggests a different course of action to remedy the situation and prevent recurrence. The first suggests removing the individuals in question (a policy adopted by the armed forces). The second suggests changing the culture of the group or eliminating the group (a policy subsequently adopted by the government). The third suggests ameliorating structural problems to reduce or eliminate the conditions surrounding the incidents.

These responses are not mutually exclusive; a successful response will include elements of all three. This study has been concerned with the third — the structural context of the Somalia mission. Although it is not the purpose of this study to pass detailed judgement on the Belet Huen incidents involving members of the CARBG, a permissive cause of the incidents was the surge in demand for deployable units for Yugoslavia and Somalia and the consequent exacerbation of the chronic overstretch of Canada's limited military capabilities. While the necessary and immediate causes of the Belet Huen incidents lie at the individual or group level, an appreciation of the larger structural context can inform efforts to prevent future incidents of this nature.

AFTER SOMALIA: CANADA AND UN PEACE OPERATIONS

Peace Enforcement and Continued Fiscal Constraints

Canada's Long-Term Fiscal Situation. A core issue affecting Canadian participation in UN peace operations, and any Canadian foreign policy activity generally, is cost. Like many traditional peacekeeping contributors, Canada is experiencing a financial squeeze of major proportions.

This has several related consequences. First, government expenditures come under increasing public scrutiny, particularly expenditures on activities outside the country, whether this be foreign aid or contributions to allies. Second, financial restraint inhibits the ability of the country to sustain the forces and the readiness required to meet the wide range of commitments, including UN operations, the government continues to maintain. Third, fewer financial resources are available to sustain such missions in the field for long periods, when in fact the nature of many UN operations necessitates long-term involvement.

While budgetary constraints have always played a prominent role in deliberations on Canadian foreign and defence policy, after the Cold War these constraints increased dramatically. The national federal debt for 1995-96 stands at an estimated $580 billion, with some 25 per cent of federal expenditures directed to interest and debt servicing. In addition, provincial debt stands at an estimated $220 billion and municipal and other debt at an estimated $20 billion. Canada's total debt is therefore about $820 billion and growing, a figure larger than the gross domestic product.

Consequences for the Defence Budget. The pressure is on present and future governments to reduce deficits, and defence, traditionally regarded as a discretionary funding sector, will not escape. For example, defence spending for fiscal year 1992-93 was $12.3 billion (about 8 per cent of government expenditures), but this accounted for some 37 per cent of the federal government's operating and capital expenditures — the single largest discretionary spending component in the budget and therefore an obvious target for cuts.[13] The defence budget has suffered a succession of cuts. The defence budget for 1994-95 was $11.8 billion, and this will decline to $9.25 billion in 1998-99. Between 1993-94 and 1998-99, defence expenditures will have fallen by more than 20 per cent.[14] Table 5.1 illustrates the steady decline in the national defence department's budget.

Table 5.1
Defence Budget Reductions, 1993-94 to 1998-99

Fiscal Year	*Defence Budget* ($ millions)
1993-94	12,034
1994-95	11,801
1995-96	11,0 7
1996-97	10,555
1997-98	9,786
1998-99	9,252[15]

The Canadian public have been generally supportive of such cuts.[16] Claims that Canada's defence capabilities have been cut to the bone, however true, are unlikely to find a broadly receptive audience in government or the public. In addition, the Department of National Defence is expected to absorb the costs of peacekeeping and humanitarian assistance operations, which are both unexpected and expensive, and divert resources away from other projects and operations. This lean fiscal climate will make the tasks of matching military means to foreign policy ends just as difficult, if not more difficult, than it has been in the past.

Canada Still Over-Extended

Persistence of the Overstretch Problem. Canada continues to face operational concerns with respect to the demands placed on the Canadian forces. In the past year, the number of Canadian troops deployed abroad has declined, relieving the immediate pressure on the army's expeditionary capacity through 1994-94 (see Table 5.2).

Table 5.2
Canadian Peace Operation Deployments

Operation Personnel as at:	31 December 1994	30 June 1995	31 October 1995	31 January 1996
UNTSO	14	14	13	13
UNFICYP	2	2	2	2
UNDOF	213	214	214	214
UNIKOM	5	5	4	4
UNCRO		1209	435	
UNPROFOR	2148	844	830	
UNPF				21
UNTAES				33
UNOMOZ	4			
UNPREDEP		1	1	1
UNMIH	29	600	595	558
UNAMIR	396	128	110	110
Total	**2811**	**3017**	**2204**	**956**[17]

However, the underlying causes of the overstretch problem remain in place. The Canadian forces continue to be committed to a wide range of contingencies. Perhaps more than any other service, the Canadian army is under pressure from demands on its resources and shrinking fiscal outlays. Although overseas deployments have fallen off in 1995, and the current situation is more manageable, the ability of Land Forces Command to sustain even a moderate surge in the number of overseas commitments without serious effectiveness and morale problems is in considerable doubt. Deployable land force assets will be in increasingly short supply, with the expected number of regular infantry battalions expected to shrink to seven in 1994-95.[18] With the government reaffirming its commitment to troop contributions in support of UN operations, however, and the involvement of Canada in operations such as I-FOR in the former Yugoslavia, the pressure on the Canadian forces to maintain land force units available for overseas deployment will remain intense.[19] In other words, despite the recent contraction in the number of personnel Canada maintains in expeditionary missions, the structural conditions of an overstretched armed forces remain in place. Currently, even regular force battalions must be brought to full strength by drawing volunteers from other units. In addition, if specialized capabilities are required, they are often drawn from other formations. Regular force units have also been compelled to draw on reservists, and while these personnel have performed well, there are concerns about the overall effectiveness of units composed of a significant percentage of reservists. As a result, the army is reluctant to increase the reserve component of the contingents it sends overseas.

It is unlikely, therefore, that Canada would be capable of deploying more than the current two battle groups allocated to peacekeeping missions, with a third available for short periods. If budget cuts continue, the number of operational units may be reduced further or the preparedness of existing units curtailed. Finally, Canadian land force units continue to be double-tasked — made available in principle to both UN operations and other contingencies. While this double tasking is less of a concern after the Cold War — alliance obligations in Europe are less likely to be activated — maintaining a wide range of tasks places more pressures on training and preparedness.

Peace Enforcement and Equipment and Training Requirements

Equipment for More Dangerous and Diverse Missions. The deployment of Canadian personnel into the 'less permissive' environments that characterize peace enforcement operations requires equipment that has not been regarded as peacekeeping 'kit' in most missions in the past. These missions require a heavier armoured capability to protect troops from a variety of light support weapons and mines, to provide mobile support weapons, and for improved mobility over country and poor roads. These missions also require heavier firepower, in the form of infantry support weapons and tube artillery. The capacity to destroy specific targets such as tanks, bunkers, and snipers at long ranges is also increasingly important, requiring mobile precision-guided weapons and specialized counter-sniper capabilities. In addition, the increasing importance of conducting operations in built-up areas and at night requires specialized equipment and training. Furthermore, the requirement to handle civil unrest and rioters raises the issue of whether the Canadian forces should be equipped with riot control equipment (such as tear gas and water hose equipment) and other non-lethal technologies. The ability to track and identify weapons that have breached ceasefire agreements requires airborne or land-based radar. The importance of the information and counter-propaganda dimension may require the acquisition of powerful radio broadcast equipment. The increasing reconstruction component of peacekeeping also will place ever-increasing demands on Canada's army engineer component and the equipment and resources devoted to it. In short, the multi-component nature of contemporary peace operations in hostile environments has demanded and will continue to demand a wider range of equipment and capabilities, both military and non-military. This has (and will) continue to increase the costs and size of deployments, as these requirements demand more lift and support capabilities.

Training for More Dangerous and Diverse Missions. The foundation for developing effective peacekeeping contingents continues to be general-purpose combat training. The base that training provides — discipline, technical knowledge and responsibility — is essential for the conduct of peacekeeping and peace enforcement operations, particularly those in less permissive environments. However, the diverse nature of contemporary peacekeeping is placing greater demands on the breadth of knowledge and training of military personnel.[20] Some in Canada have raised the issue of the extent to which training for the specifics of peacekeeping should or should not become a greater part of the preparation of Canadian forces units for service abroad and a greater part of Canada's contribution to peacekeeping in general.

As Canadian contingents encounter a widening range of functions and as tasks proliferate, so must training and expertise. The response will have to be twofold: first, Canadian military personnel will have to be trained in a variety of additional functions, and supplementary support will have to be brought in from the non-military sector. New and enhanced supplementary training for military personnel would include mediation and conflict management techniques, training in crowd control and riot control, detainment and processing of prisoners, and civil/military co-operation. Specific-to-mission training may require more rigour with respect to information about complex internal conflicts, especially on the historical, cultural, and general contextual dimensions of the conflict. The increased level of knowledge among all ranks concerning the contextual dimension must be accompanied by a clear understanding of the implications of their actions — or inaction — for the success of the mission.

In addition, training should be regarded as a Canadian contribution to peacekeeping. The Pearson Peacekeeping Training Centre is built on the concept of a new peacekeeping partnership among military, NGO and civilian components. Training and liaison activity are being performed by Canadians on special visits overseas to countries seeking to learn from the Canadian experience. In the field, the training of local constabularies and technical and medical personnel can be an important contribution to the overall success of a mission. Accordingly, assets such as the Pearson Peacekeeping Training Centre and activities such as liaison and training programs should be maintained.

Canada, Peace Enforcement, and the United States

Getting Too Close? For Canada and other countries that saw value in peacekeeping as an activity separated from the great powers, the increased involvement of the United States and the great powers in peacekeeping and peace enforcement may signal the end of one of the valued qualities of the enterprise — an activity or league all their own. For Canada, peacekeeping was an international activity that was largely independent of the United States and had the added bonus of being a morally upstanding one. In operations where the United States is present, however, particularly when they involve the use of force, Canada risks the perception (both domestically and internationally) of being linked excessively to U.S.-led actions. This is not always a bad thing, but in cases where Canadian peacekeeping experience suggests certain courses of action, while U.S.

operational doctrine or policy decisions suggest another, the political and operational ramifications may be quite severe. In Haiti and in the Gulf War, the conduct of political and military operations under U.S.-led missions did not prove especially problematic in this regard. In Somalia, however, there was considerable friction between the United States and other national contingents (though not Canada's). Canada should be wary of the long-term impact — both in Canada and on the UN — of conducting peacekeeping missions under U.S. auspices In the view of some, the UN's capacity to act as an effective conflict management instrument is already compromised by the dominance of the United States and the west in the Security Council. Despite the importance of the United States in the conduct and success of many contemporary UN operations, dependence on the United States would not bode well for the future.

Public Support: Will the Reservoir of Good Will Run Dry?

Public Support and Peacekeeping's Time of Troubles. Canada has always maintained a firm commitment to traditional peacekeeping. The concept is entrenched not only in public perceptions of the role of Canada's armed forces and foreign policy, but also in the outlook, careers, and experience of Canada's foreign policy and military establishments. The nature of peace enforcement operations is very different from the Canadian experience, however, and such operations are very different from what the public understands peacekeeping missions to be. Although a March 1993 Environics Research poll indicated that 68 per cent of Canadians thought that it was very important for Canada to participate in international peacekeeping activities, continued public support cannot be taken for granted.[21] The conflicts in which Canadian peacekeepers are now operating seem enormously intractable, with little or no prospect of peaceful resolution. With no peace to keep, Canadians see their soldiers caught in a war zone, subject to daily hardships and risks and even outright abuse, and even as they recognize the effort to alleviate suffering, they wonder about the role of the soldiers and the advisability of a continued presence.

The open-ended nature of the commitment is also a concern. There have been domestic critics of the Cyprus operation, in which Canadians served, until recently, on a continuing basis since 1964. Yet the Cyprus operation was largely peaceful; the prospect of a long-term presence in Bosnia is something entirely different. The increased risk of casualties in these less permissive environments must also be a concern. Canada has already sustained more than 80 deaths in peacekeeping operations since the end of the Cold War, although the majority of these have occurred through accident, not hostile action. The relationship between casualties and public support for peacekeeping operations is not clear, but increased casualty rates cannot be ignored in the face of a lack of progress on the resolution of conflicts. Losses can be sustained more readily if they occur in the context of progress toward peace. Beyond the worthiness of sacrifice to help others, they seem less meaningful if no progress toward peace is being made.

CANADA AND UN PEACE OPERATIONS: OPTIONS FOR THE FUTURE

The Alternatives for Canada

Given the changes in the nature of peacekeeping and the fiscal situation confronting Canadian policy makers, what choices does Canada have with respect to the future of its peacekeeping policy? As in many other countries, the end of the Cold War led to reappraisals of foreign and defence policy, and peacekeeping has been an important, perhaps even leading, subject of debate. Canada, like other traditional peacekeeping countries, has several options. Canada may choose to reduce its peacekeeping obligations with the ultimate aim of ceasing its involvement in such operations. Alternatively, Canada could decide to maintain its present commitment as a firm supporter of traditional peacekeeping and its peacemaking cousin. Or Canada might adopt a selective policy, establishing some means of restricting or reducing its involvement to certain roles or certain kinds of contingencies.

Option 1: Leaving the Game. Canada could decide to forsake peacekeeping altogether. At a time when peacekeeping operations have changed in nature and when the country faces financial problems, peacekeeping might be re-evaluated as an expensive foreign policy luxury. The relevance of peacekeeping after the Cold War would be cast into doubt, in terms of its relationship to Canadian security and Canadian foreign policy goals. With the increasing hollowness of the middle-power conception, peacekeeping might be a casualty of a more modest Canadian approach to its role in international politics. Canada would continue to support the UN and other multilateral organizations but with far less energy and expenditure of resources.

Although this approach might appeal to some Canadians, it is difficult to imagine the government arriving at such a decision. As discussed earlier, Canada continues to derive security and foreign policy benefits from its participation in UN peace operations. Furthermore, as recent events in Bosnia Herzegovina and Somalia attest, Canada will continue to be called upon by its friends and allies to participate in international contingencies and peacekeeping and peace enforcement missions.

In addition, public pressure to address human suffering will continue to prompt political action, including participation in peacekeeping and peace enforcement efforts. For political reasons, then, an abstention policy may not be attainable. In addition, with the decline of traditional Cold War political and military roles, future governments may be more, rather than less, disposed to UN peace operations and contingency missions as a means of asserting an international, multilateral role for Canada. Trends would seem to point to this. Canada has participated in each of the 15 new peacekeeping operations mounted since 1988, although its string of participation in every UN peace operation was recently broken.[22] In addition, in the 1993 election campaign, the Liberal party committed itself to peacekeeping as a priority, and this was subsequently confirmed.[23] Canada also participated in the international coalition mustered against Iraq and in I-FOR in the former Yugoslavia. In short, Canada does not have a record of refusal. Finally, to withdraw from peacekeeping would compromise another pillar of Canadian foreign policy: support for the UN and other international institutions.

Option 2: Peace Operations as a Cornerstone. On the other hand, Canada could place UN operations at the very centre of its security and foreign policy framework. Not only would Canada continue its long and proud tradition of participation in UN operations, but it would take steps to enhance its capability to contribute to such missions. This would be achieved through increases in defence spending and/or the restructuring of the armed forces for peacekeeping missions. In effect, Canada would place a larger share of its foreign and security policy eggs in the peacekeeping/peace enforcement basket.

This approach has two serious shortcomings. First, Canada has many other security and foreign policy interests, and to focus energy and resources on UN peace operations — to the detriment of interests in Europe or Asia or other issues such as proliferation or arms control — would not serve Canadian interests. Second, a restructured armed forces, designed for UN peace operations, might be incapable of performing other missions if called upon to do so.

Option 3: Staying the Course. Alternatively, Canada could continue to follow its current approach. Peace operations would continue to be identified as an important component of Canadian global activity and one of the roles assigned to the armed forces. Canada would continue to commit forces to UN operations to the limit of its capabilities, but with no substantial increases in funding for the forces and no major changes in the criteria for Canadian involvement. Should demand outstrip the availability of Canadian resources, Canada would be compelled to decline to participate in some missions.

The problem with this approach is the need to reconcile the idea of continued participation with the reality of a decline in Canada's fiscal resources and its military capability. With the armed forces already overstretched and budget cuts offering no hope for relief, Canada's ability to respond to calls for contributions of troops and materiel will be increasingly limited. Although some improved flexibility might be achieved by reducing the time between mission rotations or expanding the role of the reserves, these solutions have already been put in place and are at best improvisational and at worst damaging to morale and efficiency.

Option 4: Picking and Choosing. Canada also has the option of adopting a more selective approach to participation in peacekeeping missions. Canada would abstain from involvement in certain UN operations while choosing to become involved in others. However, if Canada is to be more selective with respect to the peacekeeping duties it undertakes in the future, some criteria must be established for selecting the missions in which Canada will participate. Establishing a discriminatory or selective peacekeeping policy will require a coherent basis for judging where to participate.

Alternative 1: The National Interest. First, the government could choose to embark on peacekeeping or peace enforcement operations only when Canada's national interests are at stake. This would be a strongly utilitarian perspective, but it could potentially have wide appeal, in that it would establish a firm link between Canadian peacekeeping and the protection of assets of political or economic importance to Canada. In essence, it aims to obtain some clear return on Canada's peacekeeping investments. In this sense, peacekeeping operations might be easier to explain or justify to the public, as the reasons for involvement would be clearer and more concrete.

To do this, however, a definition of national interests is required, and this definition must be detailed enough to specify local or regional interests that would justify participation in one peace operation but not another. For a country like Canada, it is difficult to conceive of such interests as distinct from Canada's general interests in peace operations. If the establishment of an international foreign policy role for Canada after the Cold War can itself be called a 'national interest', as this study suggests, then the utilitarian aspects of national interest as a criterion erode somewhat; the activity of peacekeeping or peace enforcement itself becomes a national interest to the extent that it supports a foreign policy role for the country. If 'role' is not conceived of as a national interest, then peacekeeping becomes dissociated from foreign policy conceptions designed to secure a foreign policy niche, an important matter for small or middle powers such as Canada and many traditional contributors to UN operations. Finally, using a selective strategy on the basis of national interest removes an important moral aspect of peacekeeping: the duty and obligation of states to respond to international crisis and human suffering. Political pressure to become involved in an operation is more likely to arise from this source than from sentiments based on national interest.

Alternative 2: Traditional Peacekeeping Only. A second selective strategy would be to get involved only in traditional peacekeeping operations — those clearly mandated and operated by the UN and that meet the conditions of partiality, consent, and force disposition. In essence, Canada would turn away from peace enforcement operations and involve itself only in operations consistent with its Cold War peacekeeping experience. This approach to selectivity would also be more consistent with Canada's military capabilities and experience. Just as important, it would be more consistent with Canada's fiscal constraints. It would also have the effect of insulating Canada's peacekeeping activities from the potential quagmires and casualties of peace enforcement operations and the impact that public reaction might have on Canadian involvement in all UN missions.

This argument, however, ignores the fact that it is precisely the large-scale peace enforcement operations that are attempting to grapple with the most important and most serious international contingencies. In abstaining from these operations, Canada would remove itself from involvement in the most prominent instances of international co-operation to control or manage violence. This approach could be criticized as a recipe for defection — Canada shirking its responsibilities to the UN and to multilateral peace enforcement efforts.

Alternative 3: Peacekeeping Without the Great Power(s). Alternatively, Canada could be selective on the basis of peacekeeping partners. Canada could choose to participate only in missions in which middle and small powers were taking part, in a kind of traditional peacekeepers' league. Canada could also choose not to become involved in operations in which the United States or the great powers played a prominent role in executing a mission. This would preserve the value of peacekeeping as an enterprise distinct from close ties to great power interests or close links to U.S. policy. It does not necessarily mean that Canada would not become involved if the United States (or other great powers) were involved in some way; Canada might still choose to participate. Nevertheless, if an operation was, for example, largely American in conception and execution, or if it depended heavily on U.S. political and operational guidance, Canada would abstain from involvement.

This policy may not be the least bit practical. The reality is that contemporary UN operations often lean on the United States or the great powers for diplomatic and resource support. In addition, concerns that motivate the United States to action may also motivate Canada; U.S. dominance of decision making and forces did not prevent Canada from involving itself in the Gulf War, for example.

Alternative 4: Choosing Niche Roles. A final way of bridging the gap between widespread political commitments and reduced capabilities is to develop alternative models of contributing. Some future Canadian contributions to UN missions could consist of smaller, more symbolic contingents of specialized support personnel, aircraft, or naval vessels. In short, Canada's contribution of battalion group-sized units would be less frequent, and more contributions would consist of smaller commitments with more specific functions designed to demonstrate Canada's political commitment to the UN effort. Canada would be selective on the basis of the operational role it fulfils in peacekeeping or peace enforcement activities.

Canada could, for example, choose to deploy communications assets and radio station capabilities, headquarters staff and equipment, medical or field support services, or language services. Canada could also supply civilian police and legal and technical civilian staff and experts. Canada would in effect seek to carve out functional niches for itself within peacekeeping or peace enforcement efforts. In doing so, Canada would not forsake the contribution of infantry contingents when these were available. However, as the availability of these contingents is reduced, Canada would still be able to contribute important military and civilian technical assets to UN operations. As the tasks undertaken by UN missions have expanded, and as the nature of conflict continues to change, the importance of these specialized capabilities will continue to increase. Success in future UN operations will rely not only on the availability of high-quality infantry units but on the presence of a number of specialized capabilities.

Providing such capabilities — communications, information, and media assets, headquarters personnel and equipment, engineering capabilities, medical capabilities, mine clearing expertise, training of local constabularies, maintenance of order functions, to name a few — becomes more prominent in an overall contribution approach or strategy for UN operations. Canada does not have a large supply of such specialized capabilities, however, either in the armed forces or in the civilian sector. Furthermore, contributions of high-quality troops are highly valued and sought after during the establishment of a UN mission. Canada's reputation as a committed peacekeeper might therefore suffer as the size of its contributions declined, and it might have less influence at the political level as a result. Nonetheless, such niche roles offer Canada an opportunity to participate in UN operations when no regular troop formations are available for expeditionary missions at the time in question.

The Consequences. Many of these options would be feasible methods of adjustment for Canada and other traditional peacekeeping countries. The most likely course for Canada is that the government will try to stay the course, maintaining participation in a wide range of peacekeeping and peace enforcement missions. At the same time, the government will have to concede that various constraints will prevent Canada from contributing to all future UN operations. If the government moves toward developing a greater capacity to contribute certain niche capabilities, it will have the option of offering some contribution during times when no infantry formations are available, without exerting counter-productive demands on land force units.

Strengthening Canada's capacity to contribute niche capabilities to UN peace operations offers an attractive solution to the pressures created by Canada's commitment to the UN, the unforeseen contingencies and demands that commitment creates, and Canada's constrained fiscal and military resources. Other countries are likely to respond differently, basing their peacekeeping strategies after the Cold War on one or more different options. This implies that in the not too distant future, the traditional contributors to UN operations will offer their contingents to the UN on a variety of bases and with different aims and goals in mind. To the extent there was ever a traditional peacekeeping fraternity, the end of the Cold War may break up that fraternity, and the motivations and aims that inspired the informal rules and conventions of traditional peacekeeping will fragment, as countries adjust their peacekeeping policies to accommodate change. This may have negative implications for the future of UN missions, particularly if many countries adopt policies of abstention or selectivity based on national interest, or if some countries contribute only to traditional peacekeeping missions, as they are safer and potentially less costly. Such options are not in Canada's interests.

CHAPTER SUMMARY

1. Peacekeeping had a strategic rationale in Canada's Cold War security policy. It contributed to the containment and resolution of conflicts that might have escalated into a superpower confrontation that would have threatened Canada.
2. After the Cold War, Canada no longer has an overarching strategic rationale for engaging in peacekeeping or peace enforcement. However, Canada's general foreign policy interests in peacekeeping remain relevant.
3. The Canadian experience in Somalia has been overshadowed by the death of Somalis at the hands of members of the CARBG. Although structural factors, in the form of the overstretch of the armed forces, did create the conditions in which these incidents took place, the immediate, necessary, and efficient causes of the incidents lie elsewhere.
4. The experience in Somalia highlighted a number of implications of peacekeeping and peace enforcement operations for Canada:

    - Fiscal realities will act as a constraint on Canada's peacekeeping capabilities in the future.
    - As a result, Canada's armed forces are, and will continue to be, stretched to the limit in terms of deployable capabilities, especially troops.

- The changing nature of peacekeeping will require new equipment and enhanced supplementary training for Canadian forces personnel.
- Canada must be aware of the implications of involvement in U.S.-led peace operations.
- The Canadian public's support for peacekeeping may erode if peace operations are seen as unsuccessful or if casualties escalate.

5. Canada should begin to adopt specialized mission roles and functions for UN peacekeeping operations, both civilian and military. This does not mean that Canada will cease to contribute troops. It means that in the face of fiscal and resource constraints, the ability to deploy specialized personnel and capabilities will allow Canada to participate in missions when regular infantry units are not available.

CHAPTER SIX

Conclusions

GENERAL SUMMARY AND CONCLUSIONS

Core Arguments Made and Central Lessons Highlighted

The First Lesson: Peace Enforcement Operations are Qualitatively Different from Traditional Peacekeeping Operations. This study has sought to clarify the distinctions between traditional peacekeeping operations and peace enforcement operations. The study argued that the evolution of traditional peacekeeping was influenced or conditioned by several structural factors, most notably the constraints of the UN system, the political constraints imposed on that system by the Cold War, and the nature of international conflict in the post-war world.

Peacekeeping may have been an improvised activity, but it reflected a set of systemic constraints and the practical compromises that were required to overcome them. The result was a conflict management instrument that relied on the consent of the parties, was lightly armed, non-hostile and impartial, and was deployed in support of a peace that was already in place. However, as the UN became engaged in conflicts where such conditions could not be met, the mandates, methods, and means of traditional peacekeeping proved unsuitable.

The UN then tried to improvise, increasing the size and scope of its involvement, escalating its use of force, and contracting out to the United States (Somalia) or regional organizations (Yugoslavia). There were no doctrines, modalities, or established conventions of operation in place. As a result, the UN was operating at first in an inappropriate conceptual space, trying to apply the conventions of traditional peacekeeping to a very different setting, then in a conceptual vacuum, as it tried to adapt its efforts to new conditions. In the absence of a coherent conceptual plan, the UN began to rely increasingly on uses of force that were not effectively linked to a larger political framework or process. The UN then lost the basis of its effectiveness as a conflict management instrument: the support of the warring factions, its impartiality, and the distinctiveness of its presence as a non-combatant party.

The principal lesson to be drawn from this examination of the genesis of peacekeeping is that the enterprise of peacekeeping, like any conflict management instrument, reflects both the political environment and the conflict environment in which it is developed. If a conflict management instrument — such as traditional peacekeeping — is applied to a situation that differs from certain proscribed characteristics, it will be unsuited to the problems at hand. Major changes in the political environment or conflict environment require new concepts and modes of operation, which must be established and in place to be successful.

A Second Lesson: The Character of International Conflict Continues to Evolve, with Implications for Conflict Management. Since the end of the Second World War, changes in the nature and style of warfare have continued to challenge prevailing war-fighting doctrines and conflict management techniques. The decolonization experience and the development of insurgency warfare were one such challenge, while the character of contemporary ethnic, religious, and factional warfare is another challenge. These conflicts take place within, rather than among states, are very localized, with a poor distinction between combatant and non-combatant, and reflect deep historical and cultural factors. They are characterized by small-unit operations, often outside political control, and tend to be prolonged struggles.

It should be taken as a given that the nature and style of warfare will continue to evolve. As a result, conflict management efforts will also have to adjust and be prepared for a wide range of possible developments. Such developments might include some combination of the following:

- the spillover of current conflicts, requiring preventive deployments;
- the outbreak of revolutionary wars between states and sub-state groups, requiring conflict management between governments and revolutionary movements, or between revolutionary factions;
- the frequent outbreak of ethnic, religious, and factional conflict originating in poverty, environmental degradation, and the political, economic, and social collapse of states;
- the use of chemical or biological weapons, requiring both defensive measures and decontamination efforts;
- the use of high-technology weapons and heavy support weapons (particularly missiles), requiring defensive countermeasures or pre-emption;

- terrorist attacks on countries contributing to conflict management efforts, requiring higher levels of domestic security;
- the use of disinformation and propaganda to discredit conflict management efforts, requiring improved information dissemination and counter-propaganda capabilities;
- the use of terrorist or urban guerrilla techniques, by factions opposed to conflict management efforts requiring improved operational security;
- the incitement of riots, requiring improved crowd control and non-lethal weapons capabilities; and
- the use of intimidation, threats, and henchmen by local officials or organized crime to coerce local populations to resist efforts toward peace or reconciliation, requiring more effective policing capabilities.

Peacekeeping or interventionary personnel will come under a wider range of threats, and these threats will not necessarily be confined to the local theatre but may extend to the home territory of contributing countries as well. This is because of the increasing tendency of one or more factions in a conflict coming to regard the UN and its contingents as a hostile force, rather than a neutral peacemaker.

A Third Lesson: Traditional Peacekeeping is Not Irrelevant or Obsolete. Despite the high profile of peace enforcement operations, traditional peacekeeping remains a valuable conflict management instrument in suitable situations and environments. Unfortunately, the highly publicized troubles encountered by UN peace enforcement operations have also stained traditional peacekeeping efforts and the UN itself.

Governments and publics in contributor countries must be reminded of the effectiveness of traditional peacekeeping missions under certain conditions. A misinformed association of peace enforcement missions with traditional peacekeeping missions could compromise the future of what has been an effective conflict management instrument.

A Fourth Lesson: The More Multi-Component the Mission, the More Diverse the Requirements. To respond to internal ethno-religious conflicts, a new instrument was required. No model or doctrine existed for a new instrument, so the UN was compelled to improvise, just as traditional peacekeeping itself had been an improvisation. The UN attempted to build on existing peacekeeping conventions by buttressing UN missions with broader mandates authorizing a wider range of actions, including the application of force, that could be used to secure the mission's objectives. UN missions became larger and less dependent on universal consent, contingents were more heavily armed and used force with greater frequency, and a wider variety of tasks were undertaken. These missions were deployed without a peace in place; part of their mission was to try to establish a peace. In addition, some UN missions took on national reconstruction or peace-building roles, which represented a qualitative change from the more limited developmental scope and breadth of earlier missions.

The lesson of this development is that in the future, irrespective of whether UN missions are mounted under traditional peacekeeping or peacemaking precepts, UN personnel will be performing a much wider array of tasks than they did in the past. Broader and more numerous mission tasks require a change in the composition of peacekeeping forces. Military personnel will continue to be crucial. However, these personnel will be performing a wider range of tasks that will demand enhanced functional capabilities and training. Furthermore, UN missions will require the increasing involvement of civilians and NGOs and, above all, a higher level of co-ordination between military and civilian elements.

A Fifth Lesson: The Dangers of Overambition. The UN effort in Somalia illustrates the dangers that can befall any mission that has extremely far-ranging and long-term goals. In Somalia, the UN was attempting to mediate between the factions while deploying military force to buttress political agreements, aiding relief operations, and engaging in national reconstruction. Within Somalia, this led to unrealistic expectations of what the UN would be able to achieve, while outside Somalia it established a set of unreasonable criteria on which to evaluate success.

Somalia demonstrated the inherent limitations of the UN, especially with respect to funding, expertise, and the support of member states. Greater attention must be paid in the future to establishing mission goals that are attainable in light of the UN's fiscal and material resources and the commitment of member states to that mission.

A Sixth Lesson: The Importance of an Integrated Political and Military Concept of Operations. The Somalia case study reveals the hazards inherent in any failure to develop a clear operational concept for the conduct of a mission, one that establishes a clear relationship between the political environment, mission goals, mission mandates, and means. In Somalia, the UN was learning and adapting as the mission progressed. The result was escalating mandates, the UNITAF operation, different conceptions of mission aims among contributing countries, and an effort to use military force in the absence of a clearly established political formula understood among the UN contributors and Somalia's factions. The UN mission in Somalia lacked the focus and coherence required to match ends with means and to establish guidelines for operating in such an unstable and dangerous environment.

A Seventh Lesson: The Dangers of the Use of Force. One of the most important lessons of the Somalia experience is the dangers inherent in a more robust application of force by a UN mission, particularly when a larger political framework is not in place or is unclear. Force was misapplied by the UN in Somalia. Firepower was deployed without a requisite level of selectivity and discrimination. This had the effect of turning local sentiment against the UN in several instances, and this led to the increasing perception of the UN as a participant (and for some, a justifiable target) in the conflict. This in turn compromised the UN's ability to act as a sufficiently neutral third party in political conflict management efforts.

On the ground, this conceptualization of UN personnel as 'enemies' or 'hostiles' removed barriers shielding UN personnel from mistreatment or attack. In such an environment, UN personnel react understandably; they in turn regard the locals as 'enemies' and undertake efforts to protect themselves, efforts that serve to undermine further their status as neutrals and reinforce or create a seige or war-zone mentality.

Somalia demonstrated how the use of force can undercut the foundation of the larger political mission of the UN in such conflicts. This is not to argue that force cannot be a useful and effective instrument in many circumstances. However, force must be applied only in a discriminate and calibrated fashion, in support of a coherent political framework, to avoid compromising the overall political position of the UN and local perceptions of the status of a mission.

Implications for the Investigation into the Belet Huen Incidents

This study identified three possible levels of explanation for the incidents involving members of the CARBG in Somalia. First, an individual level explanation would regard the incidents as the result of the misconduct and personal qualities of the few soldiers involved. A group level explanation would regard the incidents as the result of a culture inside the CAR that cultivated group loyalty, racism and indiscipline, and resistance to change. A structural level explanation would regard the incidents as the result of factors concerning the nature of the mission and the environment encountered by the Canadian Armed Forces as a whole. This study has sought to explore only the extent to which the structural level had any bearing on the incidents involving members of the CARBG.

The study concludes that structural factors in the form of the overstretched nature of the Canadian Armed Forces did contribute to the permissive causes of the incidents in Somalia. However, structural factors were not the necessary, sufficient, or efficient causes of the incidents. The central explanations for these incidents lie at the individual or group level of analysis, not at the level of structure.

Implications for Canada and Future UN Peace Operations

While the end of the Cold War removed the strategic rationale for Canada's peacekeeping endeavours, it did not remove the foreign policy rationales. Peacekeeping remains a valuable enterprise for Canada. However, the demands of UN peace operations — in terms of their frequency and intensity — led to the overstretch of the Canadian Armed Forces with respect to their expeditionary capabilities. Although the demands placed on the land forces have been reduced recently, the government's standing commitment to the UN, coupled with shrinking defence budgets, means that the structural conditions of overstretch remain in place.

This study suggested that while Canada should continue to participate in a broad range of UN missions, including peace enforcement operations, its capacity to contribute troops to expeditionary missions will continue to be limited and will come under pressure again in the future. The broader range of tasks being conducted by UN missions provides an opportunity for Canada to furnish specialized military and civilian personnel and capabilities to UN operations when regular infantry units are not available. Canada should not turn away from contributing battalions or battle groups to UN missions. When such units are not available, however, Canada should take steps to establish a capability to send smaller numbers of specialized personnel to perform certain important functional or niche roles in UN peace operations. The study also suggested that the Canadian forces enhance their supplementary peacekeeping training and improve unique-to-mission training, particularly with respect to social and cultural factors and the implications of individual actions in these social and cultural environments.

A FINAL WORD

As indicated in the introduction and executive summary, this study has sought to do more than merely describe the changed character of many contemporary UN operations. To this end, the study has reached a number of conclusions based on an examination of the changing nature of armed conflict, the changing nature of peacekeeping efforts, the lessons specific to the experience of Somalia, and the relevance of these developments for Canada. The study therefore has a descriptive and a prescriptive component. The descriptive component of the study intends to inform; the prescriptive component intends to provoke thought about future missions. To the extent the incidents at the centre of the Somalia Inquiry's mandate were caused by structural factors, a recognition of the need to alleviate these conditions and account for possible threats and obstacles in future environments will assist in anticipating and preparing for future challenges. This will reduce the prospects that misunderstanding, misapplication of techniques or capabilities, the development of suspicion and hostility between locals and UN personnel, and ad hoc, improvisational solutions to difficult problems will contribute to the future mistreatment of UN personnel or the mistreatment of local peoples by UN personnel.

Notes

INTRODUCTION AND EXECUTIVE SUMMARY

1 The author is a post-doctoral research fellow at the Institute of International Relations, University of British Columbia. The views expressed in this study are those of the author.

CHAPTER ONE — TRADITIONAL PEACEKEEPING DURING THE COLD WAR

1 See *Postwar Foreign Policy Preparation, 1939-1945*, Department of State Publication 3580 (Washington: Government Printing Office, 1949). For an examination of the origins of the UN see Robert C. Hildebrand, *Dumbarton Oaks: The Origins of the United Nations and the Search for Postwar Security* (Chapel Hill, N.C.: University of North Carolina Press, 1990).
2 Among the agencies created were the United Nations Conference on Food and Agriculture (the predecessor of the Food and Agriculture Organization) and the United Nations Relief and Rehabilitation Administration.
3 For a review of the evolution of the UN see Adam Roberts and Benedict Kingsbury, *Presiding Over a Divided World: Changing UN Roles, 1945-1993* (Boulder, Colorado: Lynne Rienner Publishers, 1994).
4 See *Charter of the United Nations and Statute of the International Court of Justice* (New York: United Nations), p. 2 [hereafter, *Charter*].
5 *Charter*, article 2/4, p. 2.
6 *Charter*, p. 11.
7 *Charter*, p. 11.
8 *Charter*, p. 2.
9 Inis L. Claude, Jr., *Swords into Plowshares: The Problems and Progress of International Organization*, fourth edition (New York: Random House, 1984), p. 72.

10 For a brief discussion of the themes and issues of Security Council reform see Paul Kennedy and Bruce Russett, "Reforming the United Nations", *Foreign Affairs* 74 (September/October 1995), especially pp. 60-62. For larger treatments of the issue of UN reform see Eric Fawcett and Hanna Newcombe, eds., *UN Reform: Looking Ahead After Fifty Years* (Toronto: Science for Peace, 1995); and Wendell Gordon, *The United Nations at the Crossroads of Reform* (Armonk, N.Y.: M.E. Sharpe, 1994).
11 *Charter*, pp. 4-5.
12 The Charter does not give the UN, however, or any organ of the UN, responsibility for making this determination. See Edwin M. Smith and Michael G. Schechter, *The United Nations in a New World Order*, Monograph Series No. 6 (Claremont, California: The Keck Center for International and Strategic Studies, 1994), p. 54.
13 General Assembly Resolution 2625 (XXV), 24 October 1970, Annex. This resolution went on to state that "Every State has the duty to refrain from organizing, instigating, assisting or participating in acts of civil strife or terrorist acts in another state". Quoted in Adam Roberts and Benedict Kingsbury, *Presiding Over a Divided World: Changing UN Roles, 1945-1993*, Occasional Paper Series (Boulder, Colorado: Lynne Rienner Publishers, 1994), p. 35.
14 See *Charter*, article 33/1, p. 8.
15 *Charter*, p. 9.
16 Quoted in Inis L. Claude, Jr., *Swords into Plowshares*, p. 75.
17 *Charter*, article 47/1, p. 10.
18 For a brief discussion of the MSC see Eric Grove, "UN Armed Forces and the Military Staff Committee: A Look Back", *International Security* 17 (Spring 1993), pp. 172-182. For a related work see Eugene V. Rostow, "Should Article 43 of the United Nations Charter be Raised from the Dead?" *McNair Paper* 19 (Washington, D.C.: National Defense University, July 1993).
19 See Abba Eban, "The U.N. Idea Revisited", *Foreign Affairs* 74 (September/October 1995), p. 39.
20 Collective security arrangements are based on the principle that members will respond as a collective in the event of aggression from any other member. Collective defence arrangements are based on the principle of alignment against a specific actor that is excluded from membership in the collective defence arrangement. Collective defence is the principle behind traditional alliances.

21 See Evan Luard, *The United Nations: How it Works and What it Does*, second edition (New York: St. Martin's Press, 1994), p. 54.
22 See Robert W. Gregg, "The Politics of International Cooperation and Development", in Lawrence S. Kinkelstein, ed., *Politics in the United Nations System* (Durham, N.C.: Duke University Press, 1988), p. 115.
23 For histories of the League see F.P. Watters, *A History of the League of Nations* (London: Oxford University Press, 1967); and F.S. Northedge, *The League of Nations: Its Life and Times, 1920-1946* (Leicester: Leicester University Press, 1986).
24 For general surveys of peacekeeping see Alan James, *Peacekeeping in International Politics* (New York: St. Martin's Press, 1990); William J. Durch, *The Evolution of UN Peacekeeping: Case Studies and Comparative Analysis* (New York: St. Martin's Press, 1993); and *The United Nations and the Maintenance of International Peace and Security*, United Nations Institute for Training and Research (Dordrecht: Martinus Nijhoff, 1987).
25 Neither operation is entered on the official UN peacekeeping or observer mission lists. See *United Nations Peace-keeping* (United Nations Department of Public Information, 1993).
26 See the Pearson Peacekeeping Centre's *Peacekeeping and International Relations* 24 (May/June 1995), p. 13.
27 See Paul F. Diehl, *International Peacekeeping* (Baltimore: Johns Hopkins University Press, 1993), p. 28.
28 The legal basis of peacekeeping has been discussed elsewhere; for a brief discussion see Phillipe Kirsch, "Legal Aspects of Peacekeeping", in *Peacekeeping: Norms, Policy and Process*, Proceedings of 1993 Peacekeeping Symposium (Toronto: Centre for International and Strategic Studies, York University, 1993), pp. 63-70.
29 *United Nations Peace-keeping*, p. 3.
30 An exception to this was the United Nations Peacekeeping Force in Cyprus (UNIFCYP), which was deployed before a political settlement to avert the risk of war. Mediation efforts began after the force was in place.

CHAPTER TWO — THE CHANGING NATURE OF INTERNATIONAL CONFLICT

1 The first estimate is taken from Bruce Russett and Harvey Starr, *World Politics: The Menu for Choice* (New York: Freeman, 1990), p. 165. The second estimate is taken from Nicole Ball, "Demilitarizing the Third World", in Michael T. Klare and Daniel C. Thomas, eds., *World Security:*

Challenges for a New Century (New York: St. Martin's Press, 1994), p. 216. Estimates are of course subject to the lack of accurate casualty lists and population data.
2 Russett and Starr, p. 165.
3 See Russett and Starr, p. 165, and William Nestor, *International Relations: Geopolitical and Geoeconomic Conflict and Cooperation* (New York: Harper Collins, 1995), p. 261; and United Nations Development Program, *Human Development Report* (New York: Oxford University Press, 1994).
4 See Ann Fremantle, ed., *Anthology of Mao's Writings* (New York: Mentor, 1971); Vo Nguyen Giap, *People's War, People's Army: The Viet Cong Insurrection Manual for Underdeveloped Countries* (New York: Vintage, 1963); and Lawrence Freedman, ed., *War* (Oxford: Oxford University Press, 1994), especially pp. 310-363.
5 For a review of the development of counterinsurgency doctrine see Michael T. Klare and Peter Kornbluh, eds., *Low-Intensity Warfare: Counterinsurgency, Proinsurgency, and Antiterrorism in the Eighties* (New York: Pantheon, 1988).
6 There are of course exceptions to this generalization. The British military has a long history and well developed expertise in counterinsurgency techniques.
7 See Charles W. Kegley, Jr., and Eugene R. Wittkopf, *World Politics: Trend and Transformation*, fifth edition (New York: St. Martin's Press, 1995), p. 430.
8 See Kegley and Wittkopf, *World Politics*, pp. 123-132.
9 See Thomas F. Homer-Dixon, "Environmental Scarcities and Violent Conflict: Evidence from Cases", *International Security* 19 (Summer 1994), pp. 5-40.
10 See Kegley and Wittkopf, *World Politics*, p. 458.
11 Raimo Vayrynen, "Towards a Theory of Ethnic Conflicts and their Resolution", inaugural lecture by John M. Regan, Jr., Director of the Joan B. Kroc Institute for International Peace Studies, University of Notre Dame, 15 March 1994.
12 For a detailed model of ethnic conflict see Ted Robert Gurr and Barbara Harff, *Ethnic Conflict in World Politics* (Boulder, Colorado: Westview Press, 1994).
13 Ted Robert Gurr, *Minorities at Risk: A Global View of Ethnopolitical Conflicts* (Washington, D.C.: United States Institute of Peace Press, 1993).
14 See Kegley and Wittkopf, *World Politics*, pp. 465-466.

Notes for pages 35–46

15 James B. Seaton, "Low-Level Conflict", *Society* 32 (November/December 1994), p. 11.
16 See Max G. Manwaring, ed., *Uncomfortable Wars: Towards a New Paradigm of Low Intensity Conflict* (Boulder, Colorado: Westview Press, 1991); and V. D. Hanson, *The Western Way of War: Infantry Battle in Classical Greece* (New York: Knopf, 1989).
17 This point has been emphasized by Martin van Creveld, *On Future War* (London: Brassey's, 1991); and John Keegan, *A History of Warfare* (London: Hutchinson, 1993.)
18 J.M. Beach, "Confronting the Uncomfortable: Western Militaries and Modern Conflict", *GeoJournal* 34 (October 1994), p. 148.
19 See C.D. Lane and M. Weisenbloom, "Low-intensity Conflict: In Search of a Paradigm", *International Defense Review* 1 (1990).
20 Beach, "Confronting the Uncomfortable", p. 149.
21 See Trevor Dupuy, *Future Wars* (London: Sidgewick and Jackson, 1992). For a review of contemporary case studies see Lori Fisler Damrosch, ed., *Enforcing Restraint: Collective Intervention in Internal Conflicts* (New York: Council on Foreign Relations Press, 1993).
22 Beach, "Confronting the Uncomfortable", p. 149.
23 See Martin C. Libiki, "The Mesh and the Net: Speculations on Armed Conflict in a Time of Free Silicon", *McNair Paper* 38 (Washington, D.C.: National Defense University, 1994).

CHAPTER THREE — THE CHANGING NATURE OF PEACEKEEPING

1 For a general review see Karen A. Mingst and Margaret P. Karns, *The United Nations in the Post-Cold War Era* (Boulder, Colorado: Westview Press, 1985). For a brief account of some of the items on the UN Agenda see Ingvar Carlsson, "Roles for the UN in International Security after the Cold War", *Security Dialogue* (26 March 1995), pp. 7-18; and *The United Nations in its Second Half-Century*, Report of the Independent Working Group on the Future of the United Nations (1995).
2 John Gerard Ruggie, "The U.N.: Wandering in the Void", *Foreign Affairs* 72 (November/December 1993), pp. 26-31.
3 Barry Buzan, "Third World Regional Security in Structural and Historical Perspective", in Brian L. Job, ed., *The Insecurity Dilemma: National Security of Third World States* (Boulder, Colorado: Lynne Rienner, 1992), p. 79.
4 Among the neo-realists see, for example, John J. Mearsheimer, "The False Promise of International Institutions", *International Security* 19/3

(Winter 1994/95), pp. 5-49; Joseph M. Grieco, *Cooperation among Nations: Europe, America, and Non-Tariff Barriers to Trade* (Ithaca, N.Y.: Cornell University Press, 1990); and Grieco, "Anarchy and the Limits of Cooperation: A Realist Critique of the Newest Liberal Institutionalism", in Charles W. Kegley, Jr., ed., *Controversies in International Relations Theory: Realism and the Neoliberal Challenge* (New York: St. Martin's Press, 1995), pp. 151-171. For examples of the neo-liberal approach, see Robert O. Keohane, *After Hegemony: Cooperation and Discord in the World Political Economy* (Princeton: Princeton University Press, 1984); Keohane, *International Institutions and State Power: Essays in International Relations Theory* (Boulder, Colorado: Westview Press, 1989); and John G. Ruggie, ed., *Multilateralism Matters: The Theory and Praxis of an International Form* (New York: Columbia University Press, 1993).

5   For general reviews of UN reform see Eric Fawcett and Hanna Newcombe, eds., *United Nations Reform: Looking Ahead After Fifty Years* (Toronto: Science for Peace, 1995); Wendell Gordon, *The United Nations at the Crossroads of Reform* (Armonk: M.E. Sharpe, 1994); and David Steele, *The Reform of the United Nations* (London: Croome Helm, 1987).

6   For a review of UN reform proposals see Richard Lee Gaines, "On the Road to a Pax U.N.: Using the Peace Tools at our Disposal in a post-Cold War World", *NYU Journal of International Law and Politics* 25 (Spring 1993), especially pp. 567-587. See also Theo Sommer, "Fifty Years of the United Nations: The Vain Dream of Peace", *Deutschland* 3 (June 1995), pp. 10-14; and Paul Kennedy and Bruce Russett, "Reforming the United Nations", *Foreign Affairs* 74 (September/October 1995), pp. 56-71.

7   See, for example, Steven R. Ratner, *The New UN Peacekeeping: Building Peace in the Lands of Conflict after the Cold War* (New York: St. Martin's Press, 1995); Thomas G. Weiss, ed., *The United Nations and Civil Wars* (Boulder, Colorado: Lynne Rienner, 1995); James Sutterlin, *The United Nations and the Maintenance of International Security: A Challenge to be Met* (Westport, Conn.: Praeger, 1995); Robert B. Oakley et al., eds., *The Professionalization of Peacekeeping: A Study Group Report* (Washington, D.C.: United States Institute of Peace, 1994); Charles Dobbie, "A Concept for Post-Cold War Peacekeeping", *Survival* 36 (Autumn 1994), pp. 121-148; and Eugene V. Rostow, "Should Article 43 of the United Nations Charter Be Raised From the Dead?" McNair Paper 19 (Washington, D.C.: National Defense University, 1993).

8   For an examination and set of proposals tabled by the Canadian government on improving the UN's rapid reaction capability see *Towards*

a Rapid Reaction Capability for the United Nations, Report of the Government of Canada (September 1995).

9 The term peacemaking has been criticized as well. See Jarat Chopra, "Back to the Drawing Board", *Bulletin of the Atomic Scientists* (March/April 1995), p. 31.

10 The term second generation peacekeeping is discussed in John Mackinlay and Jarat Chopra, *A Draft Concept of Second Generation Operations* (The Watson Institute, Brown University, 1993).

11 Traditional peacekeeping operations include first generation peacekeeping operations involving interposition or observer missions, while second generation peacekeeping operations involve multi-dimensional tasks aimed at creating a long-term settlement. See Michael W. Doyle's introduction in *Peacemaking and Peacekeeping for the Next Century*, Report of the 25th Vienna Seminar (New York: International Peace Academy, 1995).

12 For comparative discussions of the changed nature of peacekeeping see Marrck Goulding, "The Evolution of United Nations Peacekeeping", *International Affairs* 69 (1993), pp. 451-464; and Adam Roberts, "The Crisis in UN Peacekeeping", *Survival* 36 (Autumn 1994), pp. 93-120.

13 Thomas G. Weiss, "The United Nations at Fifty: Recent Lessons", *Current History* (May 1995), p. 223.

14 The new mission has been described as an effort to deter, dissuade, and deny (D3). See John G. Ruggie, "The U.N.: Wandering in the Void", *Foreign Affairs* 72 (November/December 1993), p. 29.

15 Boutros Boutros-Ghali, "Beyond Peacekeeping", *NYU Journal of International Law and Politics* 25 (Fall 1992), pp. 115.

16 See "World's Smallest Mine Defies UN", *Jane's Intelligence Review Pointer* 2 (August 1995), p. 1. For an examination of the general mine problem see "Assistance in Mine Clearance", Report of the Secretary General (6 September 1994), A/49/357.

17 For a detailed examination of the changing nature of peacekeeping see Mats R. Berdal, "Whither UN Peacekeeping?: An Analysis of the Changing Military Requirements of UN Peacekeeping with Proposals for its Enhancement" *Adelphi Paper* 281 (October 1993), especially pp. 6-25.

18 Boutros-Ghali, "Beyond Peacekeeping", pp. 115.

19 For a discussion of regional confidence building see Michael Krepon et al., eds., "A Handbook of Confidence-Building Measures for Regional Security", Handbook No. 1 (Henry M. Stimson Centre, 1993).

20 Boutros Boutros-Ghali, *Agenda For Peace: An Independent Survey of the Violence in South Africa* (Geneva: United Nations, 1992), p. 25.

138   Notes for pages 54–62

21 See John Ruggie, "The United Nations: Stuck in a Fog Between Peacekeeping and Enforcement", in William H. Lewis, ed., *Peacekeeping: The Way Ahead? McNair Paper* 25 (Washington, D.C.: National Defense University, 1993).
22 See "Peacekeeping Operations Summary", *Peacekeeping and International Relations* 24 (November/December 1995), p. 13.
23 Figures for January 1996 from "Peacekeeping Operation Summary", *Peacekeeping and International Relations* 25 (January/February 1996), p. 13.
24 See Christopher Wren, "The UN's Master Juggler", *New York Times*, 8 December 1995, p. C1; Paul Knox, "UN Faces Drastic Staff Cuts", *The Globe and Mail*, 6 February 1996; and Barbara Crossette, "U.N. Juggles Funds to Stay Afloat, Expert Says", *New York Times*, 13 September 1995, p. 7. The United States now owes $1.23 billion U.S., up from $1 billion in 1993. See Paul Lewis, "United Nations Is Finding Its Plate Increasingly Full but Its Cupboard is Bare", *New York Times*, 27 September 1993. The UN regular budget for 1996-97 is $2.68 billion U.S.
25 In 1993, only a $194 million U.S. peacekeeping payment from Japan enabled the UN to meet the September 1993 payroll.
26 Quoted in Paul Lewis, "United Nations Is Finding Its Plate Increasingly Full but Its Cupboard is Bare", *New York Times*, 27 September 1993.
27 See Thomas G. Weiss, David P. Forsythe, Roger A. Coate, *The United Nations and Changing World Politics* (Boulder, Colorado: Westview Press, 1994), pp. 76.
28 Randolph Ryan, "Can the UN keep peace?" *The Boston Globe*, 19 June 1993.
29 For a microcosm of this debate see "Peacekeeping: Two Views", *World Affairs* 155 (Spring 1993), pp. 143-155. See also Willie Curtis, "The Inevitable Slide into Coercive Peacemaking: The US Role in the New World Order", *Defense Analysis* 10 (1994), pp. 305-321.
30 For a review of the contents of the presidential decision directive, see Eric Schmitt, "U.S. Set to Limit Role of Military in Peacekeeping", (continues as, "U.S. Completes Policy to Limit Military Role in Peacekeeping" on p. 5) *New York Times*, 29 January 1994, pp. 1, 5.
31 For a detailed examination of peacekeeping and human rights see "Peacekeeping and Human Rights", *Amnesty International* (January 1994) IOR 40/01/94.
32 Thomas G. Weiss, David P. Forsythe, Roger A. Coate, *The United Nations and Changing World Politics* (Boulder, Colorado: Westview Press, 1994), especially pp. 72-82.

139   Notes for pages 62–73

33 See Carlsson, "Roles for the UN in International Security", p. 9.
34 Weiss et al., *The United Nations and Changing World Politics*, pp. 73.

CHAPTER FOUR — THE UNITED NATIONS AND SOMALIA:
LESSONS AND IMPLICATIONS

1 For general histories of Somalia see I.M. Lewis, *A Modern History of Somalia: Nation and State in the Horn of Africa*, revised edition (Boulder, Colorado: Westview Press, 1988); Helen Chapin Metz, ed., *Somalia: A Country Study*, Country Studies/Area Handbook Program (Washington, D.C.: Federal Research Division, Library of Congress, 1993); Lee V. Cassanelli, *The Shaping of Somali Society: Reconstructing the History of a Pastoral People, 1600-1900* (Philadelphia: University of Pennsylvania Press, 1982); and David D. Laitin and Said S. Samatar, *Somalia: Nation in Search of a State* (Boulder, Colorado; Westview Press, 1987). See also Ernest Harsch, "Somalia: Restoring Hope", *Africa Recovery Briefing Paper* 7 (15 January 1993).
2 The Darod make up 35 per cent of the population, the Hawiye 23 per cent, the Isaaq 23 per cent, the Dighil and Rahanwyn 11 per cent, and the Dir 7 per cent. The Sab have traditionally been a subordinate group in Somali society, although this distinction is fading.
3 See Michael Maren, "Somalia: Whose Failure?" *Current History* 95 (May 1996), pp. 201-205.
4 See Jeffrey Clark, "Debacle in Somalia: Failure of the Collective Response", in Lori Fisler Damrosch, ed., *Enforcing Restraint: Collective Intervention in Internal Conflicts* (New York: Council on Foreign Relations Press, 1993), pp. 209-211.
5 By the late 1980s, Barre was called 'the mayor of Mogadishu' because his control extended no further than the area immediately around the city.
6 See Samuel M. Makinda, *Seeking Peace from Chaos: Humanitarian Intervention in Somalia*, International Peace Academy Occasional Paper Series (Boulder, Colorado: Lynne Rienner Publishers, 1993); and Helen Chapin Metz, ed., *Somalia: A Country Study*, Country Studies/Area Handbook Program (Washington, D.C.: Federal Research Division, Library of Congress, 1993).
7 There is some dispute in the literature about the link between the clans/sub-clans and the political movements. See James Wyllie, "Somalia-State Disintegration and Regional Stability", *Jane's Intelligence Review* 5 (February 1993), pp. 71-72; Jarat Chopra and Åge Eknes Toralu Nordbø, "Fighting for Hope in Somalia", *Peacekeeping and Multinational*

Operations, No. 6 (Norwegian Institute of International Affairs, 1995), p. 26; and *Managing Arms In Peace Processes: Somalia.* Disarmament and Conflict Resolution Project, United Nations Institute for Disarmament Research (New York: United Nations, 1995).
8 See James Wyllie, "Somalia — The Bitter Struggle Resumes", *Jane's Intelligence Review*, 6 (September 1994), pp. 410-411.
9 See *The Economist*, 16 August 1992, p. 2.
10 "Somali leader calls on foreign troops to withdraw", *The Montreal Gazette*, 20 September 1992.
11 See Makinda, *Seeking Peace from Chaos*, p. 43.
12 See Harsch, "Somalia: Restoring Hope", p. 11.
13 For a brief review of the humanitarian situation in Somalia at this time see Boutros-Ghali's report to the Security Council on the situation in Somalia, UN Security Council Document S/23829/Add. 1, 21 April 1992.
14 These NGOs included the International Committee of the Red Cross, Save the Children Fund, CARE, World Vision, Oxfam, Médecins sans frontières, Concern, and others.
15 See Clark, "Debacle in Somalia", p. 238.
16 UN and aid NGOs issued repeated warnings about conditions in Somalia throughout 1990-91. The UN's World Food Program had warned of a potential famine in Somalia in December 1990.
17 See UN Security Council Resolution 733, 23 January 1992.
18 See UN Security Council Resolution 751, 24 April 1992. The observer contingent was not approved by General Aideed until 21 June 1992, as Aideed initially refused to allow the personnel to be in uniform, insisting that they wear civilian attire instead.
19 See UN Security Council Resolution 767, 27 July 1992.
20 See UN Security Council Resolution 755, 28 August 1992, and "Report of the Secretary-General on the Situation in Somalia", UN Security Council Document S/24480, 24 August 1992.
21 African Rights, drawing on information from CARE and the U.S. Centers for Disease Control, reported that the famine had passed its peak by November 1992. See Matthew Bryden, "Somalia: The Wages of Failure", *Current History* 94 (April 1995), p. 148.
22 "Force needed to aid Somalis, UN leader says", *The Globe and Mail*, 1 December 1992.
23 See UN Security Council Resolution 794, 3 December 1992.
24 These sectors centred around Mogadishu, Baledogle, Baidoa, Hoddur, Bardera, Kismayu, Belet Huen and Jailalassi.

141   Notes for pages 80–83

25 See *UN Chronicle* 30 (March 1993), p. 16.
26 This divergence was later recognized by Boutros-Ghali, when he stated that UNITAF was working to achieve security, while the UN was working on the political and humanitarian issues. See Harsch, "Somalia: Restoring Hope", p. 5.
27 In Boutros-Ghali's view, the heavy weapons of the organized factions were to be "neutralized and brought under international control", and the weapons of the local "irregular forces and gangs" were to be confiscated and destroyed. See *Security Council Document S/24992*, 19 December 1992, p. 7.
28 For a detailed account of the disarmament effort in Somalia see *Managing Arms In Peace Processes: Somalia*, Disarmament and Conflict Resolution Project, United Nations Institute for Disarmament Research (New York: United Nations, 1995).
29 See *Report of the Commission of Inquiry Established Pursuant to Security Council Resolution 885 (1993) to Investigate Armed Attacks on UNOSOM II Personnel which Led to Casualties Among Them*, S/1994/653 (1 June 1994), p. 13.
30 The United States would also retain considerable influence in UNOSOM II: the commander, Turkish General Cevik Bir, was nominated by the United States, and the deputy force commander Major-General Thomas Montgomery, and the Secretary-General's Special Representative, Admiral Jonathan Howe (Ret'd.) were Americans.
31 This cost estimate led to considerable discussion in the Security Council. See UN Security Council Document S/25354/Add. 1, 11 March 1993.
32 See Security Council Document S/25354, 3 March 1993, p. 19.
33 Quoted in Mark Fineman, "Tough Task still faces UN force in Somalia", *The Ottawa Citizen*, 4 May 1993.
34 The document was entitled the "Addis Ababa Agreement of the First Session of the Conference on National Reconciliation".
35 This agreement was entitled "Agreement Reached between the Political Leaders at the Consultations Held in Addis Ababa, 30 March 1993".
36 In a country with a strong oral tradition and a literacy rate of 30 per cent, the radio was a vital source of information and communication.
37 See UN Security Council Resolution 837, 6 June 1993.
38 A Commission of Inquiry to investigate armed attacks on UNOSOM II personnel, established by UN Security Council Resolution 885 on 16 November 1993, concluded that a war had existed between Aideed's forces and UNOSOM II and that while the attacks on UNOSOM II personnel were premeditated and unjustified, recommended that the

effort to disarm the factions in Somalia be discontinued. See *UN Security Council Document S/1994/653*, 1 June 1994.

39 Poor co-ordination and readiness had a role in the heavy casualties suffered by the army rangers early in October. See Eric Schmitt, "Reinforcements for U.S. Troops Delayed 9 Hours", *New York Times*, 6 October 1993. For broader criticisms see also Shawn H. McCormick, "The Lessons of Intervention in Africa", *Current History* 94 (April 1995), pp. 162-166; and Matthew Bryden, "Somalia, the Wages of Failure", *Current History* 94 (April 1995), pp. 145-151.

40 Final U.S. casualty figures were 30 dead and 175 wounded. See The Pearson Peacekeeping Centre, *Peacekeeping and International Relations* 24 (March/April 1995), p. 16.

41 The national reconciliation effort, based on the Addis Ababa agreement of 27 March 1993 and the Nairobi Declaration of 24 March 1994, never succeeded in the aim of establishing a long-term peace process.

42 See UN Security Council Document S/26738, 12 November 1993, especially pp. 22-24.

43 See UN Security Council Resolution 897, 4 February 1994.

44 See UN Security Council Resolution 954, 4 November 1994.

45 Nine UN agencies and 38 NGOs will remain in Somalia to carry out humanitarian efforts.

46 For a rare argument on the successes of the Somalia experience see Chester A. Crocker, "The Lessons of Somalia: Not Everything Went Wrong", *Foreign Affairs* 74 (May/June 1995), pp. 2-8.

47 Quoted in Richard C. Longworth, "Phantom Forces, Diminished Dreams", *Bulletin of the Atomic Scientists* (March/April 1995), p. 25.

48 For an excellent account of the strategic and tactical implications of consent see Dobbie, "A Concept for Post-Cold War Peacekeeping", pp. 121-148.

49 Lessons-Learned Unit, Department of Peacekeeping Operations, Friederich Ebert Stiftung (Life and Peace Institute, Norwegian Institute of International Affairs), *Comprehensive Report on Lessons Learned from United Nations Operation in Somalia (April 1992-March 1995)* (December 1995).

50 Chopra and Nordbo, "Fighting for Hope in Somalia", p. 101.

51 See Christopher C. Coleman and Jeremy Ginifer, *An Assessment of UNOSOM, 1992-1995: A Seminar Report* (Lessons-Learned Unit, Department of Peace-keeping Operations, and the Norwegian Institute of International Affairs UN Program, 1995), p. 13.

143   Notes for pages 92-99

52 This is a problem not only with respect to the United States. Boutros-Boutros Ghali criticized Italy for taking action in Somalia outside UN command and following orders from their capital (because of concerns about casualties). See "Italy seeks halt to peacekeeper's fighting", *The Globe and Mail*, 13 July 1993.

CHAPTER FIVE — PEACEMAKING, THE SOMALIA EXPERIENCE, AND CANADA

1 See Joseph T. Jockel, "Canada and International Peacekeeping", Significant Issues Series 16 (Washington, D.C.: Center for Strategic and International Studies, and Toronto: Canadian Institute for Strategic Studies, 1994), p. 11.
2 For an effective review of Canadian involvement in peacekeeping see Alex Morrison, "Canada and Peacekeeping: A Time for Reanalysis?", in David B. Dewitt and David Leyton-Brown, eds., *Canada's International Security Policy* (Scarborough: Prentice Hall, 1995). See also Alex Morrison, ed., *The Changing Face of Peacekeeping* (Toronto: Canadian Institute of Strategic Studies, 1993); and House of Commons, Standing Committee on National Defence and Veterans Affairs, *The Dilemmas of a Committed Peacekeeper: Canada and the Renewal of Peacekeeping* (June 1993).
3 These themes were raised consistently, though with varying degrees of emphasis, in Canada's white papers on defence. See *White Paper on Defence* (Canada: Department of National Defence, 1964), pp. 6, 10-16; *White Paper on Defence* (1970), pp. 3-7; and *Challenge and Commitment: A Defence Policy for Canada* (1987), pp. 4-7.
4 Special Joint Committee of the Senate and the House of Commons on Canada's International Relations, *Independence and Internationalism* (Ottawa, June 1986), p. 34.
5 Henry Wiseman claims that peacekeeping "enhanced Canada's reputation as a middle power, [and contributed] to Canada's stature and influence in the UN". See "United Nations Peacekeeping and Canadian Policy: A Reassessment", *Canadian Foreign Policy* 1 (Fall 1993), p. 138.
6 See Department of National Defence, Chief Review Services, Program Evaluation Division, "Final Report on NDHQ Program Evaluation E2/90: Peacekeeping, 1258-77 (DGPE)" (30 June 1992). See also Jack Granatstein, "Peacekeeping: Did Canada Make a Difference? And What Difference Did Peacekeeping Make to Canada?", in John English and Norman Hillmer, eds., *Making a difference?: Canada's Foreign Policy in a Changing World Order* (Toronto: Lester Publishing Ltd., 1992).

7 The peacekeeping mission continued to be embraced by the Canadian Armed Forces. In the wake of the Cold War, peacekeeping became even more prominent as a role and rationale for the armed forces, particularly the land forces.
8 See John Ward, "Troops stretched, analysts warn", *The Ottawa Citizen*, 2 September 1992; and "MacKenzie says Canada near limit of answering UN call", *Winnipeg Free Press*, 26 September 1992.
9 See Tim Harper, "Peacekeeping: Reaching Canada's limit", *Toronto Star*, 28 November 1992.
10 See "The Jane's Defence Interview", *Jane's Defence Weekly* 14 (November 1992).
11 Also spelled Baledogle.
12 See G2 Branch, Land Forces Central Area Headquarters, *Somalia Handbook*.
13 Figures are drawn from Department of National Defence, *Making Sense Out of Dollars, 1992-1993 Edition* (1992).
14 See Department of National Defence, "Statement on Defence Budget Reductions, March 1996".
15 For these figures see Department of National Defence, "Statement on Defence Budget Reductions, March 1996".
16 See Geoffrey York, "Most Canadians favour cuts to military spending, poll shows", *The Globe and Mail*, 26 May 1993, p. A6. See also Geoffrey York, "Grits likely to sink submarine plan", *The Globe and Mail*, 8 November 1993, p. 1.
17 Figures drawn from "Peacekeeping Operation Summary", in Alex Morrison, ed., *Peacekeeping and International Relations* (Canadian Peacekeeping Press). These figures do not reflect Canadian forces deployed overseas outside of direct UN auspices.
18 See Paul Koring, "Army pushed to breaking point", *The Globe and Mail*, 27 May 1993, p. A1. Three reserve battalions will also be available, but the Canadian forces have consistently maintained that units composed of more than 25 per cent reservists are not suitable for peacekeeping duties abroad, although this policy may come under re-examination.
19 See Jeff Sallot, "Ottawa to boost overseas capability, Collonette supports UN military efforts", *The Globe and Mail*, 11 September 1995, p. 5.
20 For some proposals on peacekeeping training, see Robert B. Oakley et al., eds., *The Professionalization of Peacekeeping: A Study Group Report* (Washington, D.C.: United States Institute of Peace, 1994); and Ernest Gilman and Detlef E. Herold, eds., *Peacekeeping Challenges to Euro-Atlantic Security* (Rome: NATO Defence College, 1994).

21 See Department of Foreign Affairs and International Trade, Foreign Policy Division, *Canada and Peacekeeping: Backgrounder* (April 1994), p. 1.
22 Standing Committee on Foreign Affairs, *Meeting New Challenges: Canada's Response to a New Generation of Peacekeeping*, Report of the Standing Committee on Foreign Affairs (February 1993), pp. 4-6.
23 See *Creating Opportunity: The Liberal Plan for Canada* (Ottawa: Liberal Party of Canada, 1993), p. 106.